gyapong

Destiny

Blessed Prince Agyapong

An Eating Mouth Destroys Destiny

Speak into your life to accelerate your miracles!

Blessed Hope Publishing

Imprint

Any brand names and product names mentioned in this book are subject to trademark, brand or patent protection and are trademarks or registered trademarks of their respective holders. The use of brand names, product names, common names, trade names, product descriptions etc. even without a particular marking in this work is in no way to be construed to mean that such names may be regarded as unrestricted in respect of trademark and brand protection legislation and could thus be used by anyone.

Cover image: www.ingimage.com

Publisher:
Blessed Hope Publishing
is a trademark of
International Book Market Service Ltd., member of OmniScriptum Publishing Group
17 Meldrum Street, Beau Bassin 71504, Mauritius

Printed at: see last page
ISBN: 978-613-7-84386-4

Copyright © Blessed Prince Agyapong
Copyright © 2019 International Book Market Service Ltd., member of OmniScriptum Publishing Group

DEDICATION

I dedicate this book to three special persons.

To all the ministers of the Gospel around the world, especially those whose writings have paved a way for me.

Mrs. Henrietta Ofusu Agyapong. Thanks for being there for me always.

To my elder brother- Pro. Robert K. Agyapong.

GOD RICHLY BLESS YOU ALL

SPECIAL ACKNOWLEDGMENTS

I am indebted to the author of all inspiration, the omniscient one, the only wise God, King of Kings and Lord of Lord for His grace upon my life to put this work together.

I deeply appreciate, Arch-Bishop Duncan Williams (Action faith Ministries), Bishop. Dr. Van &Mrs. Udo Obioma{ G.O.M.I.F. president- Nigeria}, Rev. Eastwood Anaaba {F.G.M}, Bishop Clarence McClendon {U.S.A}.

Rev Owusu Ansah, and Rev.Gabriel Ansah {All of Adom F.M} ChiyereAnoshie {Nigeria}, Dr. Shadrack Ofosu ware (London). Apst. Gen. Sam korankye Ankrah, Rev. &Mrs. J.W. Sackey.
Christina Muchi, Omniscriptum manager, and Veronica Virlan, my editor, as well as the entire workers of Blessed Hope Publishing.

Table of Contents

INTRODUCTION

Someone once said who should be blamed when a leaf falls from a tree? Is it the wind that blew it away? Or the tree itself that let it goes? Or is it the leaf which grew tired of holding on? Life unfolds a lot of misunderstanding. To many that is all what life is, full of mysteries and cannot tell what will happen next. Yes, at times things fall on their own but a force is required to enforce arise.

To the believer life must not be so, because God has entrusted you with power in your mouth to determine what happens to your life. Circumstances cannot do a thing to you without your consent.

Everything God create has a specific purpose, and that is to solve a problem. Until you know the purpose of a thing it becomes a mystery to you, and you will misuse it and cause a problem for yourself instead of benefits.

Dr. Myles Munroe once said *"when purpose is not known abuse is inevitable"*. Purpose is the reason something was made, it is the end for which the means exists.

There is no area in our personality more directly related to our total well-being than the mouth. Your mouth was given to you not just for eating and drinking, even though it is good, but it was giving to you by God to chart the cause of your life.

To many, eating with their mouth and talking about others is all that they know! I am not saying that you should not eat, but there is more and higher ways for us to use our mouth. The Bible says He gives food to the eater and seed to the sewer {Isaiah 55:10}. Therefore it is either you use your mouth for eating alone or to sow seeds of words that will bring you a bright future. **You have a real problem if you eat more than you talk.** The Bible says

"…for it is a good thing that the heart be established by grace and NOT WITH FOODS which has not profited these whose who have occupied with them "HEBREWS 13:9 NKJV

Jesus also said

"It is written man shall not LIVE BY BREAD (food) ALONE but every word that proceeds out of the mouth of God" MATTHEW 4:4.

God's word is more than a guidebook or a book of instructions. **GOD'S WORD IS LIFE** (Deut 32:46-47). If the physical food can give your body strength, then spiritual food can do much. Eating only the physical food cannot help you to fulfill your destiny on the earth as a believer. And there is no food in this world that can nourish your body totally, because 80% of the foods we eat are chemicals.

God foreknow this that is why He said He will take away sickness from your food and water- Exodus 23:25-26

God, in His own wisdom designed the human head to have seven openings in three pairs, two eyes, two ears, and two nostrils. But all is restricted by the seventh openings to one (the mouth), this one gives us more blessing than all other six together. The reason for your mouth is to glorify God, to change things for your benefits and to chart the course of your life. You cannot be a real believer without being a talker. Christianity doesn't operate by an eating mouth but by a speaking mouth. A soundless Christian is a sign-less Christian. It may not be by something you had done wrong but by something you haven't done right. The world belongs to a tongue talking people. When you say what God says about you, you are functioning rightly in using your mouth for the purpose it was designed.

This is a spiritual principle in the kingdom of God. Use your mouth, for that's where the miracle is. Miracle happens when you are able to speak the right words in accordance with the things in the spiritual realm.

The purpose of this book is to show you how to get started on the road to a life of miraculous by using your mouth. The first thing you need to master in spiritual things is words. The spiritual law a few of us has realize is that our confession rules us. What you say with your mouth will affect the course of your destiny, positively or otherwise. Read it with an open heart and mind, and allow the Holy Spirit to minister to you.

Most likely, I have never met you, but I already know you are special and loved by God! I bless you with a desire to learn how to become a wonder to your generation by changing every situation with your own words.

-Blessed Prince

CHAPTER 1
WHAT IS CONFESSION?

Confession is not a formula for getting God to do something but to be aware and identify with what God has already done for you in Christ by speaking them forth
-Blessed Prince

God planned that this great salvation (eternal life) and His love should be given to the world through confession of our mouth. Christianity is called a great confession. Therefore everything we have in God's kingdom is manifest by our confession. That is why the confessors have been the only great leaders in the revolutionary life that Jesus gave to the world. The Bible says

"Let the redeemed of the Lord SAY SO, whom he has redeemed from the hand of the enemy" Psalm 107:2
....let those who love your salvation SAY CONTINUALLY, let God be magnified Psalm 70:4
Sadly, most of the confession we hear today magnified the devil. Whenever the word confession is used, some instinctively thinks of confessing sins, weakness and failures, but that is the negative side. The person who is always

confessing his sins and weaknesses is building weakness, failures and defeat into his system and comes under the supremacy of Satan. Don't misunderstand me, if you have done something wrong, confess it, but don't spend your whole life confessing wrongs.

 We need to recognize that there is more in the Bible about a positive confession than there is about a negative confession. To tell what Satan is doing in your life is to deny who you are in Christ. Our confession should witness to the truth we believe. When God saw the darkness on the face of His creation, He did not consider or say anything about the darkness. He said let there be light and without any connection there was light.

Some also thinks confession is a formula for getting God to do something for them. Confession is not just a positive talking or to make something to happen, neither it is making desperate statements to try to escape difficult situations, but it is walking in what you see in the invisible by a revelation. This is the reason some people do not get any result even though they have been confessing positively for years. Don't make them in times of crisis; make them before you need comes.

What is confession?
The word confession is from the Greek word "Homologeo" it is a compound word "Homo" means "the same" and "logeo" means "word"

- To the believer it means saying something that God says about you in spite of any situation or your circumstances.
- It is to declare openly by the way of speaking out freely a deep convict of facts of what God has said.

- It is speaking in unity or be in agreement with the word of God concerning a particular thing or the situation.
- Confession is affirming Bible truth, repeating with your lips from your heart the things God has said in His word ABOUT YOU in His word.
- It is being identified or acknowledge with the thought and language in God's plans and purpose on earth, by saying it with your mouth. The word says

"That the COMMUNICATION of thy faith may become Effectual (operative) by the ACKNOWLEDGING of every good thing which is in you in Christ Jesus" Philemon Vrs 6 OKJV

Our Christian life is based on our communication. Your faith must be communicated, and must be identified with His two fold oneness in our confession.
"He suffered shame to give us glory
He was made sin for our righteousness
He was condemned in order to justify us
He was made poor in order to make us rich
He was made sick in order that healing might be ours
He went to hell in order to take us to heaven
He became as we were, so that we might become as He is in this world (1 John 4:17)

The reason some found themselves in unpleasant situation is they have not come in terms of their identification with Christ.

The idea of confession is to speak into your life the revelation you have received from God's word. You declare what is already belongs to you in Christ and not what you are trying to get. It is re-echoing what God has said. We just speak the truth as it is in God's word. That is the only thing that can prevail in this world, where its system has been programmed to fail.

CHAPTER 2
THE IMPORTANCE OF YOUR CONFESSION

Remember that the vital side of our redemption is based upon our confession.

-Blessed Prince

The most incredible gift God has given to man is the ability to talk and to see its manifestation. *When you understand that your spirit continually produces what you speak, you will realize why some bad things happen in your life.* When God looks at you in the spirit, He sees your words. Even though God knows our thought, but He acts by our words and not by our thoughts.

There are those who think that the confession of faith is not important, they feel there must rather be an emphasis on holiness, gentleness, discipleship, patience etc. I believe those are important and they all play special roles in the life of a Christian.

However this does not mean we should play down on the importance of our faith confession. The fact that the heart is important to the body doesn't mean that kidneys or liver are not equally important, they are important, and they have special roles to play in the body.

Our redemption has two sides, the legal and the vital sides. The legal side is to know what God has done for us in Christ Jesus. But knowing only the legal side makes God's word only doctrine or formalism which is out of the reality. We need to know the vital side also, which is confessing it to become what he talks about in our lives. That is why confession is important in the life of a believer. Satan's aim is to destroy our understanding of the power and the value of our confession, because men have been given authority on the earth by their words. To know that Satan is defeated by our substitute and that his defeat is eternal makes our redemption a blessed fact and reality. Confession does several things to the believer. It locates and fixes the land marks of his life. You will never be a conqueror and enjoy the riches of grace in your redemption until you confess them. Therefore you are where you are because of your confession.

- **YOUR SALVATION DEPENDS ON YOUR WORDS NOT BY YOUR DEEDS**

"That if you shall CONFESS with your mouth the Lord Jesus, and shall believe in your heart that God hath raised Him from the dead, you shall be saved. For with the heart man believe unto righteousness and WITH THE MOUTH CONFESS IS MADE UNTO SALVATION". Romans 10:9-10.

There is no such thing as salvation without confession. You can be born in a Christian home, attend church services, and even believe in Jesus and still go to hell, when you refuse to confess Him openly. Because Jesus said "whosoever therefore shall confess me before men, him will I confess also before my father which is in heaven" (Matt 10: 32-33).

And in John 12:42-43, we have example of people who only believe Him but they did not confess Him openly. It says *"Nevertheless among the chief rulers also many believe in Him; but because of the Pharisees* **THEY DID NOT CONFESS HIM"** *Lest they should be put out of the synagogue; for they love the praise of men more than the praise of God"*.

The psalmist said **....let those who love your salvation SAY**). **CONTINUALLY....** (Ps 70:4 Which means if you love to see salvation of God in your life, say it continuously.

The question is, Why it is that our openly confession seems so important to God? It is because God does not want any secret disciple. If you believe it, you will say it. And if you have not done this before, this is the right time to do it. From the beginning to the end, whether you like it or not, true Christianity is based on our positive confessions. I know you will say that it is by believing, yes! Believing is involved but if you do not confess what you believe you still will not be saved.

- **YOUR LIFE GOES WHERE YOUR MOUTH GOES**

"You are snared with the words of your mouth, you are taken With the WORDS OF YOUR MOUTH". Proverbs 6:2

There is no place your mouth cannot talk you to. Your life circumstances are influenced on daily basis by the words of your mouth. The character of your life is the character of your words. Your life is not different from your words. What you think, believe and confess precondition your life. Your words define your life, value and personality. Your language is your life.

Your mouth can take you to heaven or hell.
By your confession, you are heal or sick
By your confession, you are weak or strong
By your confession, you are saved or lost
By your confession, you have plenty or lack
You are snared by your confession or set free
You fail or succeed by your confession
Your words are bringing increase or decrease
Your words are creating doors or walls
Your words are bridges or barricades.

The main reason God drove Adam and Eve from the Garden of Eden is not because He cannot forgive them of their sin, but to prevent them from eating the tree of life {Gen 3:24}, because if they do, there would be no way for salvation and man will become like the devil or demons permanently. The question is, where are that "two trees" which were in the Garden of Eden today? (Gen 2:9). It is connected with our tongue in the spirit.

"Death and life are in the power of the TONGUE and those who love it will eat its FRUIT". Proverbs 18:21

It is only a tree that bears fruit and the Bible says your tongue is a tree. You can have the tree of Life or the tree of Death in your life. The tree of life is also in your tongue. Now we don't need to blame Adam and Eve, because we have been eating the forbidden fruits at all time by the words of our mouth.

"A wholesome tongue is a TREE OF LIFE but perverseness (misuse) in it breaks the spirit".Proverbs15:4

Another names for the two trees are, the tree of blessing and the tree of calamity.

Do you know that Jacob killed his beloved wife Rachel whom he served for fourteen years in order to have her as his wife by his own words unconsciously? He said

"With whomever you find your gods, do not let him (that person) live...... FOR JACOB DID NOT KNOW THAT RACHEL HAD STOLEN THEM". Genesis 31:32.

The poisonous words of Jacob from his tongue killed her, because the Bible says the tongue is unruly evil, full of deadly poison (Jams 3:8).

Oh! When we come to know how words affect our lives, we will be far more careful of our words. I like how The Massage translation put proverbs 18:21, it says

"Words kill, words give life, they are either poison or fruit- you choose".

Wrong words can break the protection of God from your life. This was what happed to Job in Bible. Reading on the surface, you may think that Job suffered the entire calamity he did merely as a trial of his faith. However, Job was the one who opened the way for the enemy to attack him. The devil himself knew that Job was protected and that is why he asked God, *"Hast not thou made an hedge about him, and about his house, and about all that he hath on every side?"* (Job1:10).

Which means every child of God has a hedge of protection around them, put there by God Himself, whether they know it or not. But what was Job's confession? He said, **"I was not in safety, neither had I rest, neither was I quiet, yet trouble came" (Job 3:25).**

How could Job talk that way when even the devil knew he was protected? Because of his ignorance. And the Bible says *"He that diggeth a pit shall fall into it, and whose breath the hedge, the serpent shall bite him"* (Eccl 10:8).

The serpent is the symbolic of the devil, and Job break the hedge around his life and by his own negative words. You must realize that irrespective of what the circumstances shows you, the devil has no right and no business pulling his strings in your life; however, if you break the hedge, then you leave yourself exposed.

- **IT IS A CALL OF THE BELIEVER**

"Therefore, holy brethren partakers of HEAVENLY CALLING, consider Jesus the Apostle and the high priest of our confession". Hebrews 3:1

We are partakers of heavenly calling. The word holy brethren are the believers or anyone who has accepted Christ as his Lord and personal Savior. So what is that heavenly calling? It is to speak the word and God's will into the earth. In which way by considering (ponder or meditate) on Jesus. Thinking about Jesus make you talk like him. The Bible says

"Fight the good fight of faith, lay hold on eternal life, to which YOU WERE ALSO CALLED and have confession the good confession in the presence of many witness. I urge you in the sight of God who give life to all things, and before Christ Jesus who witness the GOOD CONFESSION before Pontius Pilate". 1Timothy 6:12-13

Your profession is to confess His words. Our confessions link us to Jesus as our high priest anytime we speak. He has made us kings and priest (Revelation 5:10). We are His associates and He is our high priest. Every believer must offer sacrifices with his mouth (Hebrews8:3), and the kings declare words of power (Eccl. 8:2). Our duty is to speak God's words on earth.

- **OUR CONFESSION HAS A RECORD BOOK IN HEAVEN.**

God records both negative and positive words we speak in heaven according to the scriptures; God is a very detailed and meticulous records keeper. He has a lot of books in heaven which will be open on the judgment day(Revelation 20:12) but there is one which is opened from time to time in His presence which is called the book of remembrance. The Bible says

"Your words have been stout against me, says the Lord. Yet you say, what have we spoken so much against you? You have said, it is useless to serve God; what profit is that we have kept His ordinance, and that we walked as mourners, before the Lord of hosts? Then those who fear the Lord spoke to one another, AND THE LORD listened and hear them to them, S0 A BOOK OF REMEMBRANCE WAS WRITTEN BEFORE HIM for

those who fear the LORD and whose meditate on His name". Malachi 3:13-14, 16.

So, what really is the book of remembrance for? It keeps the names and the record of words, especially those who talk right (confession) base on the word of God. Whenever that book is opened all our confession are released unto us. Remember that "If the clouds be full of rain, they empty themselves upon the earth" (Eccl. 11:3). Hallelujah!

- **IT PUT YOUR ANGLES TO WORK**

".......your words were heard; and I HAVE COME BECAUSE OF YOUR WORDS." Daniel 10:12

I believe in the ministry of angles. Don't let any devil confuse you about the ministry of angles; just as the demonic world is invisible, the angelic world is also invisible. But that does not mean we should worship angles. The Bible made it clear that they are our servants (Heb 1:14). And when John the revelator fell down to worship the personal angle of Jesus; the angle said **"see that you do it not, for I am your fellow servant"** (Rev 22:8-9). This shows that we don't need worship them. One of their duties is to use the words of our mouth on our behalf, either positive or negative. The Bible says

"Suffer not thy mouth to cause thy flesh to sin; neither say thou BEFORE THE ANGLE that it was an error; wherefore should God be angry at thy voice (words) and destroy the work of thine hands?" Ecclesiastes 5:6. KJV.

17

Be careful with your words. When the angle appeared to Daniel, he made a statement that I am very interested in, he said "I HAVE COME BECAUSE OF YOUR WORDS". It was not words that were spoken in Heaven that sent the angle to Daniel or put the angle of God to work. It was words spoken on earth by someone confessing in line with God's word that put the angle to work. Praise God!

- **IT OPENS THE DOOR INTO THE SUPERNATURAL.**

The greatest things that will ever happen to you will be when you move into the spiritual realm. There is a spiritual realm to enter into. Your intellect and physical senses will fight you every step of the way to keep you from moving into this realm, because if the natural mind isn't renewed by the word of God, it will hold you in the natural realm.

So many have barely taught that spiritual realm yet they do not know how to enter into that realm. Words are bridge in between the natural and the spiritual realm. Your words can open a way for you to enter into the supernatural.

CHAPTER 3
WHAT DO YOU SEE?

The performance of God in your life is determined by how clearly you can see in the spirit, God cannot give to you what you can't see

-Blessed Prince

Your ability to see in the spirit marks your maturity. Many Christians are suffering today because of their spiritual blindness. You can be cheaply robbed of whatever you cannot see. That's why God want Jeremiah to see clearly before he can perform in his life.

"Moreover the word of the Lord came unto me, Saying, Jeremiah WHAT DO YOU SEE? And I said, I see branch of almond tree. Then said the LORD to me, You have see well, for I am ready to perform my word" Jeremiah 1:11-12

God is still asking us the same question today, what do you see? The question is not what is going around you or what is the economy but what do you see? The image that God's word builds inside you can become the most powerful force in your life. That image will cause you to succeed when others fail. John G. Lake said *"every believer should enjoy the same type of ministry Jesus did while living on earth and this reality could only be accomplished by seeing themselves as God sees them".*

This is one of the great secrets of every great man of God, both in the Bible and in our days {the power of seeing}. David said "I have set the Lord always before me (Psalm 16:8). Moses did his assignment according to what he saw (Heb. 8:5). Don't leafing through the pages of the Bible as like a newspaper. The word of God can create pictures in your mind; it will show who you really are. It matters what you see. Elijah said to Elisha that you have served me with all your being for years and in truth, but you have asked a hard thing, nevertheless you will have the double portion if only you can see it (2kgs 2:10). Which means the greatest test of a believer for another dimension is the ability to see things in the spirit. What do you see?

Dr. Lillian B. Yeoman's told a story in his book "The great physician", about a famous English preacher by the name of Dr. Joseph Parker, pastor of city temple in London. As he was crossing the Atlantic by ship to minster in North America, Dr. Parker just sat on deck hour   after hours, gazing at the vast expanse of water. He seemed unaware of anything around him while others were terrifying by the surrounding water at the ocean. One young man approached him and asked "sir" what do you see there? Why are you not shaking? He smile and reply, *"I see nothing but God".*
The Bible says "Fools eyes wonder to the ends of the earth (Prov. 17:24), but to be wise is to look into the lord, so that you will be enlighten and not be shame (Ps 34:5).

AS FAR AS YOU CAN SEE

The extent of your vision is the boundary of your blessings. Abraham became the Possessor of the whole earth when God ask him to look; He knew it was not that physical land. By faith, he saw the whole world with his spiritual eyes and once he was able to see it. God said "It's yours" This was his certificate of ownership of the planet earth (Gen. 13:14-17). Life is the way you see it. The things you see with your eyes of faith and take possession in the realm of the spirit becomes realities as you speak them forth. God Himself calls Abraham a prophet (Gen. 20:7), but there's nowhere in the Bible I saw him prophesy. It is because he was able to see things which the natural eyes cannot see, being a spiritual man. He foreseen the days of Jesus and Jesus Himself confirmed it (John 8:56).

As Joshua prepared to take Jericho, the Lord said to him, **"SEE",** I have given to you the Jericho and everything in it" (Joshua 6:2). Whatever you are able to see from Genesis to Revelation is obtainable. Don't puncher your future with the traditions that leads to failure but the future that has been captured by the scriptures. You are where you are because of how far you can see.

CHANGED BY SEEING
You become what you see; you can't change for better, if you can't see well. The spirit of God can only change you into the same image you behold inside you, so it is the devil. King David advice his Solomon that "Let your eyes observe my ways" (Prov 23; 26). It is impossible to see a better life, without beholding a better thing. When you see brighter, you shine brighter.

"But we all, with unveiled face, BEHOLDING as in the mirror the glory of the Lord, are transformed into the same image from glory to glory, just as by the spirit of the Lord" II Corinthian 3:18.

Beholding is the same as looking and it came from a Greek word **"SKOPEO"**, it means to consider, mark, or take cognizance of something until that image becomes a part of your consciousness. Jesus said if you look at a woman and desire of her you have already slept with her, that is the negative side but in the positives side it means if you also look at the good things, riches, health and success and desire of it, you have already made yourself that-you transform yourself into that image, because the more you look the more you become.

The first mirror God give to Adam was his wife (Eve). He wasn't aware of what he looks like. He didn't know how his mouth looks like or the shape of his nose, eyes or his head, until he saw Eve. That is why he said in Genesis 2:23.

"And Adam said, THIS IS NOW the bone of my bone and the flesh of my flesh. She shall be called woman, because she was taken out of man"
Take a close look at this statement. Why did he start his statement with "This is now?" Because he was confuse about his own image. He knows how all the animals look like, the nose of the elephant and the monkey.
 Adam was searching for what his image looks like and when he found out, he said "this is now. It means he has finally got what he was searching for. The devil also brought his mirror through the fruit which carries his own image and presented it to Eve (Gen. 3: 6). Before everything else, she saw something. Notice that God did not say if you eat the fruit I will kill you, but He said

"In the day that you eat from it you shall surly die" (Gen. 2:17).

The devil did not tempt Eve with that fruit just because God has said they shouldn't eat that fruit. It is because the devil's image and his nature were in that fruit. After they ate that fruit, they were transformed into his image according to what they saw. "SOMETHING ALWAYS ENTERS BEFORE SOMETHING HAPPEN". But now God has brought another mirror to all men and that is the word of God. (James 1:25). Jesus was the written word made alive, now the word takes the place of Jesus as we behold His glory; we are changed into His glory and image [Greek word "Metamorphoo"]. God is rebuilding Himself in us through His word. Hallelujah

Jacob could have gone back to his father's house with an empty hand, if he didn't use this principle. It made him wiser than his wicked uncle and made him rich. His uncle made him pay for every lost sheep whether he is responsible for it or not. He reduces his wages every year for 20 years; he used to serve for just one sheep for six years. But the spirit of the lord taught Jacob the power of beholding. Jacob took rods from different trees, tie it together and place it where the flocks came to drink and as they were drinking the water and beholding it, the image of the rods enters the flocks and when they conceived they brought forth the colors of the trees.(Gen. 30:37-43).
Every image you behold forms something in you. When you see a picture of failure, sickness or poverty, say **NO!** Don't see walls, see doors (I Cor 10:13, I Pet. 1:14)

As far as your eyes can see, it shall be given unto you. But all you have seen is sickness, so it has becomes your companion, you have seen negative. That's why you are where you are, you have seen demons everywhere in all things and that has made you a demon-conscious instead of God-conscious.

The main reason the Holy Spirit was given to us is to open our eyes that we might see with His eyes, hear with His ears and understand with his heart. That's true spirituality, until you see it you are not entitled to possess it.

CHAPTER 4
NOTHING HAPPENS UNTIL YOU SPEAK

A closed mouth is a closed destiny

-Blessed Prince

Jerry Weintraub wrote a book entitle "WHEN I STOP TALKING, YOU WILL KNOW I AM DEAD". Silence doesn't mean consent; whoever said silence was golden hadn't heard of fool's gold! Silence isn't golden and it surely doesn't mean consent, so you need to say something. When you keep silence, the devil will keep you down. Prophet Isaiah said "for Zion's sake he will not keep silence" (Isa 62:1). The reason majority of Christians, though they are earnest but they are weak and failure, is because they have never dared to make a confession of what they are in Christ. God's word ought to produce results in your life, but nothing happens until you speak it. A believer whose mouth is always shut has a lot to lose. What you can't say, you can't see. Martin
Lutter king Jnr once said, *"Our lives becomes end the day we start been silence to the things that matters"*.

We determine that something is alive as long as it is able to communicate with its environment. Apostle Paul said

"And even things without life giving sound, whether pipe or harp, except they give a distinction in sounds, HOW SHALL IT BE KNOW WHAT IS PIPED OR HARPED?" 1 Corinthians 14:7. KJV

Your words will distinct you from the rest of the world, and your words show the kind of a person you are. People would rather lay the blame of their misfortune on God once they don't understand why things are not working for them. Sometimes they makes some statements that sounds so nice and very religious, like "whatever will be will be", "if it's mine, it is mine", "things for you never get lost", "if God wants things to change, He will". That's not true and such statements do not impress God. Listen, you can be sincerely wrong. He doesn't run people's life the way many of us thinks He is.

Things will not change for better unless you change them by your mouth. When you study the Bible well you will see that He has actually given to us the power to influence our own destiny.

IF YOU BELIEVE IT ENOUGH, YOU WILL SAY IT.
Your faith is not complete without saying it. Until you speak, nothing happens. It is a spiritual principle. Never give up on believing and saying. Indeed out of the abundance of the heart the mouth speaks. When the mouth is closed, it is a clear indication that the heart could be empty, half-filled or it is in a meditation mode.

"We having the same spirit of faith, according as it is written, I believed and therefore have I spoken. WE ALSO BELIEVE AND THEREFORE SPEAK".
II Corinthians 4:13

It is not enough to hear good messages or to know and read the Bible from Genesis to revelation, you have to talk it! As long as the word remains in your heart and doesn't come out of your mouth, it will not produce results, regardless of the amount of words you know. The power in it will not be released in your life until you speak it forth. May be you are reading the Bible and you came across Ephesians 1:3 which says

"Blessed be the God and the father of our Lord Jesus Christ, who hath blessed us with all the spiritual blessings in heavenly places in Christ".

He has already blessed you, invests and made a deposit in Christ for us. The question you must ask yourself is 'how these spiritual blessings can be translated into material blessings in your everyday life? The answer is simple; you will go back to the beginning and see what God did. He said 'let there be light and it was light', By His confession.

Faith confession is the "currency" you use to transfer God's provision from unseen realm of the spirit to this natural earthly realm. By your sayings you can translate it into physical realm into your life. That is why God instructed the children of Israelites to do in Deuteronomy 6: 6, 7. It says

…..**"And those words which I command you today shell be in your heart, you shall teach them diligently to your children, and shall TALK OF THEM, when**

YOU SIT in your house, and when YOU WALK by the way, and when YOU LIE DOWN, and when YOU RISE UP", and again it says *in Joshua 1:8 that "This Book of the Law shall no depart out of **THY MOUTH** ".….*

The key to prosperity and success in every area of life is to keep God's word in your mouth, this is where most people run into problem, they let the word depart out of their mouth or they really never put it in their mouth. Even God need to say it before it appears in His creation. The whole earth was chaotic, mass and full of darkness and the Holy Spirit was brooding over it, incubating upon it but nothing changed until God said something (Gen. 1:2).

If you hold your Bible up to your ear, you can't hear a sound; you are the one to give a voice to God's word for it to work in your life. Putting the Bible under your pillow but cannot give you protection from demons, putting it on your business table but cannot force your work to move forward. You can't put it on a sick person's head and expect him to get healed; you have to declare it before it works. You must say something. In the court of law, you have no choice but to speak *"Declare, that you may be justified"-Isaiah 43:26.*

It is your speak that count not your silence. You can be innocent and have all the evidence against your accuser and still go to jail when you refuse to talk. Jesus said **"FOR BY YOUR WORDS you shall be justified, and by you words you shall be condemned". Mathew 12:37**
Jesus used legal terms in this verse. He was talking about verdicts in a court of law. We know that the word "justified" means acquitted or set free to prosper in every area of life, and condemned means to be put in bondage. Even though God knows

our thought, but He acts by our words and not by our thought. The world belongs to a tongue talking people. SAY SOMETHING!

CHAPTER 5
BEFORE YOU SPEAK

(FOUNDATIONS FOR CONFESSION)

Just as every gun needs bullets, so it is to operate in the confession of the word, and no structure is stronger than its foundation

-Blessed Prince

The beginning of man trouble started by not knowing when and who to talk at the right time. When it was the right time for the man to talk, he kept silence, and when it was the right time for the woman to kept silence, she talked and we all know the outcome. Some make confessions without any foundations, and then the devil beats them badly. Their lives have become holocaust {complete destruction} which is from the Greek word "HOLOKAUSTOS". Though the Bible teaches us to confess God's word but there are things you must know before you speak. Just reciting the scriptures or pontificating day and night over the word of God without foundations, will not make it work for you. Learn how to speak every word in a manner that will work for you. The Bible says

"IF THE FOUNDATIONS ARE DESTROYED, what can the righteous do?" Psalm 11:3

You need foundations for confession. No structure can stand on its own without a foundation. We don't live by a lucky number, but by written wonder. And it is the working of the word that makes a believer a living wonder. You cannot confess or bare witness of things you do not know. The secret of confession and of dominating faith lies in getting a true understanding of what Jesus actually did for us in His word.

GET KNOWLEDGE
Ignorance has prevented many Christians today from the realm of the miraculous and the good life God has already plan for them. To live a victorious life in Christ, having revelation knowledge of God's word is indispensable. The Bible says

"Therefore my people are gone into captivity, BECAUSE THEY HAVE NO KNOWLEDGE and their honorable men are famished and their multitude dried up with thirst". Isaiah 5:13

The word did not say they are struggling because the devil is so strong or powerful, or they don't pray enough or fast enough or they are not holy or faithful, but because of the lack of knowledge. (Psalm 82:5-7). Ignorance is not the unavailability of knowledge but the refusal to acquire knowledge. The word of God has answers to everything but it is your responsibility to locate them.

I am not writing this book because I know everything. THERE IS NOTHING NEW UNDER THE SUN (Eccl. 9:1). Even Daniel himself learns from another prophet before he found out the right time for Israelites to come out of exile {Dan. 9:2}. It is your knowledge that gives your freedom {Prov. 11:9, 2Pet 1:3-4}.

And also don't be ignoramus. Know the difference; Ignorance does not know it at all, but ignoramus is to think you know it all (they do not know that they do not know). One of the great dangers we face in the Christian life is to assume that we know something when we know nothing. No matter who you are, there are things God will not tell you personal, unless you learn them from others. Jesus met Paul face to face on the road to Damascus, but He told him to go to the city for Ananias to tell him what he must do (Acts 9).

Why didn't Jesus tell him by Himself? Because God has raised men and women who are instruments of illumination and until you receive their ministry, you will remain in darkness. If you don't come in contact with men who have found what you are looking for, your search may never end!

God has given human gifts to the Body; they cannot be replaced by even the Holy Spirit. You may ask, but Blessed Prince, "Jesus said when the spirit of truth is come; He shall guide you into all truth". Good question, but this doesn't mean you should say you don't want anybody to teach you. No! There are many ways the Holy Ghost teaches us, and what is going on right now, is the Holy Ghost teaching you through His inspired words in this book. Go for knowledge.

The reason many people are stagnant in their lives is that they are stingy. How much can it cost you to buy a book or Cd's that can change your life and your love ones. You will be the same that you are this year in five years time, except for two things- the books you read and the people with whom you walk. If you are not rubbing your mind with others, it will soon become dull. No one person will ever be so spiritual that he doesn't need other people.

We all need one another. Jim Lundy said, follow, or get out of the way. The Bible says BUY THE TRUTH AND KNOWLEDGE (Prov. 23:23), but it also said wisdom is too high for a fool {Prov. 24:7}. Buy books, tapes, etc, that talks about the field you find yourself whether it is from black man or white man, success doesn't responds to colour of the skin but by accurate knowledge.

"So shall the KNOWLEDGE OF WISDOM be onto your soul, when thou hath found it, then, there shall be a reward and thy expectation shall not be cut off". Proverbs 24:14 KJV

Successful people make it a habit to learn something new in their area of interest daily. God has designed the Channel of information to be the cure for our frustration. In life, what you receive is what you conceive and what you conceive is what you bring forth.

MEDITATION

The most deeply spiritual men and women I know are people who have given much time to meditation. Meditation means to think deep on the word, it is ponder on the word until a revelation comes out of it. Meditation consists of spiritual searching of the mysteries backing the word. It is digesting the word into your spirit.

"What God want to give to you is not a job, a healing or money but the word of God in your spirit" said Pastor Chris Oyakhilome. God's word is like buckets that go deep down inside you and pull up ideas and dreams you never knew you had. This is what prophet Jeremiah said about mediation.

"YOUR WORDS WERE FOUND AND ATE THEM, and your word was to me the joy and rejoicing of my heart…" Jeremiah 15:16

There is a need for you to meditate upon the word. God told the Israelites to go the around city of Jericho for six days and on the seventh day they should shout for the walls to come down, it was a sign of meditation on the word before you speak. The Bible says

"Meditate on these things; give yourself entirely to them, that your progress may be evident to all" {1Timothy 4:15}.

Your profit will appear to all even if they don't like it, they can't deny it. No meditation, no profits, give a serious mental attention to it. *The reason for spiritual failure is to treat the word as though it were a common book. Said by E.W Kenyon.* I have already said, do not leafing through the pages of Bible as you would a newspaper, it is through intense study and meditation that the word takes root in your spirit, and becomes one with your spirit. This is where you catapult into the realm of possibilities.

PERSONALISE THE WORD

Every encounter in scriptures comes to people individually. The Bible is full of words but it is the word you appropriate and make it personal that will come to pass in your life.

"It is the spirit who gives life, the flesh profited nothing. The words that I SPEAK TO YOU are spirit, and they are life. John 6:63

Notice Jesus didn't say "the words that I speak to everybody. No! He is very specific; He says "The words that I speak unto you! He is talking to you. So when you hear any good message, statement, or preaching you can personalize it. This is what many people don't understand; when we release prophecies into the atmosphere upon the congregation, remember that nobody's name is written on it.

Therefore you can make it yours. When prophets prophesy, he does not only edify or comfort but he actually create, and it becomes a gift for anyone who want it.

The Greek word "katalambasno" means to take hold of something and make it yours. Jesus personalize the word by saying *"The volume of the book is written of me, I have come to do thy will oh God"* (Psa. 40:7, Heb10:7) also, when Jesus read the scroll of Isaiah, afterward, he closed the book and said to them. "Today this scripture is fulfilled in your ears. The Bible says, **"And all of them fixed their eyes on him"** (Luke 4:18-20) why? Because they don't know that you can personalize the word of God for yourself.

When it comes to spiritual, you only speak for yourself. Because the sweetest sound in your hear is your name. You can personalize any word in the Bible.

The word fulfilled is a Greek word "PIEROO" it means fully possess the thing until it becomes a part of you in it manifestation.

Abraham is no more, David, Solomon etc. and Jesus is also living in us now. Therefore you can personalize every word you hear; you can even write your name there, when you personalize the word, it becomes a Rhema for you. Revelation is progressive. This is the way I share the last part of grace. "Surely goodness and mercy is following Blessed Prince K. Agyapong all the days of my life, and I dwell in the presence of the Lord, prospering and living forever and ever. Amen!

A pastor got mad because someone said the God of kobby, he said that Kobby is not an Israelite; it should be the God of Abraham, Isaac and Jacob. YES, but God is not God of the dead but for the living (Matt 22:23).

The Bible says "Blessed be the God and father of OUR Lord Jesus Christ….." (Eph 1:3). This means when you are born again He is YOUR God and your father too, and you don't need to be Israelite. In Christ we are one.

"For there is no difference between the Jews and the Greek; for the same Lord over all is rich unto all that call upon him" (Rom 10:12). So there is nothing wrong when you say my God, the God of Kobby or Akosua.

When God's word comes to you, don't say "He is talking to us" No! He is talking to you! That is why Paul said "I can do all things through Christ", not we can do all things through Christ. Personalize the word for yourself. The Bible said

"So that we may boldly say, The Lord is MY helper and I will not fear what man shall do unto ME". Hebrews 13:6

He started with "that we may" and moves to "My", "l" and "me". He Personalize it. God's word is God speaking to you. It is not just the knowledge of the scriptures, it is the word that is built into you and becomes a part of you that count.

BELIEVE

"What wound have become of me, IF I HAD NOT BELIEVED to see the goodness of the lord in the land of the living". Psalm 27:13 Amp

When it comes to the things of God, until you believed nothing works for you in the land of the living. Only what you believe is allowed to happen. I BELIEVE strongly in what Smith Wigglesworth said "I would rather believe God for a minute than cry a useless cry all night. It is one thing to find the word and another thing to believe in it, mental assent admits, and admires the word but does not believe in it. God does not want the Bible readers but the Bible reading-believing Christians.

Many read about our redemption, sing about it as though it was but a fable, they don't believe it. You automatically become what you believe, you will become on the outside what you believe on the inside. No man has ever reached his highest development through unbelief. *Bruce Barton said "Nothing splendid has ever been achieved except by those who dared believe that something inside of them was superior to circumstance".* Jesus said unto him, if you can believe all things are possible to him that believes" {mark 9.23}. You don't need to a billionaire but be a believernaire.

The disciples of Jesus used every methods He uses, said every word He says, Yet they couldn't cast the demon out of the boy. Afterward the disciples asked Jesus in private "we did everything you used to do, but why couldn't we cast it out? And He told them the truth, because of your unbelief (Math.17:20).

There is no such thing as impossibility. Whatever you believe commits God to perform. "Who has believed our report? And to whom is the arm of the Lord revealed? {Isaiah 53:1}. Whose report do you believe? When you believe Doctors report, you get doctors result. When you believe peoples report, you get peoples result and when you believe God's report, you get God's result. There is no such thing as non-belief. Everyone believes something. The Israelites saw the promise land but they couldn't enter in because of unbelief. (Heb. 4:17-19.)
The root of sin started with unbelief, men belief the devil's word and disbelief God's word.

NOTICE THE TENSES OF GOD'S WORD
Your tenses become your dearest helps or your worst enemies in confession said by E.W. Kenyon. It is very important that you carefully note the tenses used as you study the Bible. God spoke in the past tense in many portions of the scriptures

"Declaring the end from the beginning and from ancient times the things that are not yet done…. Isaiah 46:10

God sees the end from the beginning that is why He speaks the end from the beginning. Abraham the father of faith took note of the way God spoke to him in Gen. 17:5 "Thy name shall be Abraham; for a father of many nations **HAVE I MADE THEE**. And at that time the man had no child! As far as God was concerned, it was already done. Abraham also apply this in his confession by calling those things which has be not as though they were and was strong in faith giving glory and thanks to God (Rom 4:17-20).

If you are going to get your heart's desire in future, it will never come. You say "I am going to get my healing or riches, I know that Christ bear my disease and my poverty and I have a right to it. It is good but that does not affect your disease or your poverty. Your tenses have taken you as a prisoner. But if you say "I know that He bear my disease, my poverty and thank Him for it and say by his stripes I am healed, by His poverty I am rich, then the tenses are working for you. Now whenever you see the word of God in past or present perfect tense. It means that in the mind of God that thing is done or that promise has been fulfilled, I don't know whether you have ever thought of it or not.

EVERYTHING IN THE SPIRITUAL REALM THAT THE BELIEVER NEEDS TO MAKE HIM SUCCESSFUL BELONGS TO HIM.

Take time and meditate in the tenses of these scriptures. John 4:4-5, John 1:12, John 5:14, I Corinth.3:21-22, 2Corinth. 5:21, Col. 1:12-13, Eph.2:6, Heb. 12:22-23, John 1:16). The word is a present-tense; it is a living voice from Heaven.

SAY IT BOLDLY

The need of the Holy Spirit was not just to speak in tongues but to speak the word in boldness. Boldness is in connection of your righteousness (Prov. 28:1). Nobody is permitted to see the manifestation of the spirit without boldly speaking (Phil. 1:14). The mark of every true prophet or minister is seen in his or her boldly speaking. Jesus says what He means in boldness and mean what He says. God told Ezekiel to have a great boldness (Ezek.3:4-10). Loyalty to God will manifest in courage and boldness.

"Now when they SAW THE BOLDNESS of Peter and John and perceived that were unlearned and ignorant men, they marveled and they took knowledge of them, that they had been with Jesus". Acts 4:13

"And he began to SPEAK BOLDLY in the synagogue, whom when Aquila and Priscilla had heard, they took him unto them and expounded unto him the way of God more perfectly" Acts 18:26

Your identification with Jesus is your boldness in His word without reservations, that is what glorifies Him {I Pet. 4:11}

God wants us to follow Him in the way of His speaking. He said it, so that we may boldly say (Heb. 13:6). Boldly confess the word not your feelings, and boldly confess your supply not your lack.

"AND NOTHING TERRIFIED BY YOUR ADVERSARIES, which is to them an evident token of perdition, but to you of salvation and that of God" Philippians1:28 0KJV.

Your terrifying speaking gives your enemy a prove that you have fail, because spirits knows if you really mean it. Don't be afraid of things you are going through, the higher it goes, the bigger it will fall before you. Someone once said you need to receive the word joyfully and forcefully apply it. Faith gives courage to confession and confession gives boldness to faith.

The secret of boldly speaking knows that the word cannot fail. You cannot be defeated by using God's words, they are eternal, and they are all-powerful. Every time we speak boldly we commit God's word integrity to manifest openly.

CHAPTER 6

IF YOU HAVE A MOUTH YOU HAVE A CHOICE

God made man a creature of choice and He respects choices

-Blessed Prince

Why isn't your life glorious? Why haven't you been able to do everything you want to do? Why aren't you filled with joy every day? The answer is, because you have a choice whether you realize it or not, every day of your life, every moment you have been making choice.

All living creatures have the privilege of making a choice, and freedom to choose is the gift from God. You do not build destiny on chance but on choice. You are sum total of the choices and the decision you make every day. You can choose to stay where you are or you can choose to move forward in life by using right words. Death and life are not in the circumstances or in the environment, neither it is in the events.

They are in what you say about the situation, and you have a mouth, therefore you have a choice.

"I call heaven and earth as witness today against you, that I have set before you life and death, blessing and cursing, THEREFORE CHOOSE life, that both you and your descendents may live". Deuteronomy 30:19

God is the best examiner who gives you the right answers, so that you wouldn't fail in life. Real choice comes by our mouth. Jesus said, say what you want to have.

"for verily I say unto YOU, that WHOSOEVER shall say to this mountain, be thou removed and be thou cast into the sea and shall not doubt in his heart, but shall believe that those things which he says shall come to pass, he shall have whatsoever he says". Mark 11:23

God doesn't deal with you on the bases of what somebody believes you to be or say about you. The truth is, in the spirit realm, it is what you say and believe that count, and not what somebody believes or says about you. The word "YOU" appeared five times in this verse which means it is your voice that God want to hear not somebody's voice on your behalf. Because He knows that the sweetest sound in a man's hears is his\her name. You may ask, Blessed Prince, but Jesus is our intercessor in heaven. Yes, but that doesn't means He is praying for us in the presence of the father, because in the spirit or in Heaven it is not done. Otherwise Jesus has contradicted Himself, But He mean what he says and says what He means. I am not trying to say you don't need someone to help you in prayers, but you lose a lot if you don't believe in your own words. Read this scripture carefully.

"In that day [The days of the church] you will ask in my name and I DO NOT SAY TO YOU THAT I SHALL PRAY (speak) THE FATHER FOR YOU. FOR THE FATHER HIMSELF LOVES YOU………..". John 16:26-27.

The intercession work of Jesus simply means, He is our representative in heaven, and we are also His representative on earth. We don't pray for Jesus but we pray in His name. What I want to say is that you need to take responsibility of your life, even If someone has cursed you, you can reverse it with your mouth. Remember that every curse is reversible but blessings cannot be reverse (Num 23:20). Know that curse operates only in the physical after the death of Christ. In fact every curse is fake, but blessings operate both in spirit and appears is physical and it is irreversible. Know that if you are a believer, you are born of the spirit and have the power to overcome every curse. Generational curse becomes ineffective in your life. Now your ancestral link can only be traced to the patriarchs of God's kingdom, like Abraham, Isaac and Jacob. These are your true ancestors and according to the Bible they were super-abundantly blessed.

There was a French prince who refused to curse; his father king Louis xvi was beheaded along with the queen, during the French revolution. When they prepared to guillotine the little prince, the crowd yelled "Don't kill him, he is so young that his soul will go to heaven and that is too good for a member of this wicked Royal family.

They announced their scheme "give the prince to the witch, she will teach him to curse. Then he will sin and when he dies, he will go to hell. For months the witch tried in vain to force the prince to curse. He would stamp his feet and refuse, asserting **"I was born to be a king and I shall never speak that way"**.

Notice that the devil is called the tempter and not a forcer. Even Jesus, God told us that, He chose the good (Isa. 7:15) and He gives everybody who come to Him the right to choose by asking them what do you want Him to do for you?

CHOOSE GOD AS YOUR BEST PARTNER

If you don't know Jesus as your Lord and Savior, this is the right time to do that. Because nobody understands, feels, cares and knows you like God does, there are things about your life that may surprise people but not God, because He knows you before He forms you (Jer. 1:5).You were with Him before you fall from Him to humanity by the fall of Adam; He knows you can't get into divinity, so He steps out of eternity in-time to be with you. Oh, how God love you! He can turn himself to be with you in every field you find yourself.

If you find yourself in the valley, He is the lilies of the valley, as an astrologist, He is the bright morning star, if you are a farmer, He says I am the vine and ye are the branches, when you are in darkness, He is the true light. If you are hungry, He is the bread of life and when you are thirsty, He is the living water. If you don't have a shepherd, He is the good shepherd. He will never leave you or forsake you. God is not mad at you. He is the C.E.O of the world. Choose God. Man's love is so fake and fraud. It comes and goes but God's love is forever.
 Remember you have no father but God (Eph. 4:6)
You have no Brother but Jesus (Heb. 2:11)
You have no companion but Holy Spirit. (John. 14:16)

CHAPTER 7
THE REALITY OF THE WORD

Your spirit can reach the point where the things in His word will became as real to you as Jesus

-Blessed Prince

You won't gain control over affairs of life until the word of God becomes real to you. This is what many have failed to see, the word has never become real to us due to the religions mindset. Jesus said "you make the word of God of non-effect because of your traditions". Reading the scriptures without the spirit of God brings only the head knowledge which cannot affect your life. ***The Bible is the most precious and wonderful gift from the Lord to his people but it was not meant to take the place of the Holy Spirit", *** *said Rick Joyner.*

The church is called to be the bride of Christ. How would any bride feels if on her wedding day her husband handed her a book and said "darling I wrote this for you so that I would never have to speak to you again" what kind of relationship would that be? The Bible deals with the general things of God and the Holy Spirit also deals with the individuals in the specific things of God. For an example, the Bible said we must work but it does not tell us the specific work we must do as individuals.

This is where the spirit of God comes in; we need both the word of God and the spirit (voice) of God. The letter kills but the spirit gives life. (I Corinth. 3:6) and you cannot also move higher by the spirit without insight of the word. There must be a balance. The spirit is there to confirm and to make the word alive in us.

"Ever learning and never able to come to the knowledge of the truth"-II Timothy 3:7.

You can read the Bible from Genesis to Revelation and still lack the revelation knowledge of the word, until the spirit gives you the insight. (Prov. 1:23). The reading of the word on its own is not what will produce results for you but understanding it, and it only comes by the spirit of God.

"But there is a spirit in the inner man and the INSPIRATION OF THE ALMIGHTY GIVETH THEM UNDERSTANDING". Job 32:8

Religion gives rules to make a deadly formalism, without the vital side which makes the word a reality, but Christianity gives life.

NOT WHAT WE SHOULD BE BUT WHO WE ARE NOW IN CHRIST

We are aware of what we have been out from, but have no idea what we have been born into. The purpose of God is not to bring us out of the power of Satan but also to bring us into the kingdom of His son. There are two things involved; one cannot make the work done.

"Then He brought US OUT from there, that He might bring US IN, to give us the land which he swore unto our father". Deuteronomy 6:23

"Who HAS DELIVERED US FROM the power of darkness and HAS TRANSLATED US INTO the kingdom of His dear Son." Colossians 1:13

The understanding of these two scriptures gives us the reality of the word. The question is where are you now? Are you still in Egypt, the power of darkness or you have been translated into the kingdom of His dear Son? Religious mindset has built walls around the word.

The Danish theologian Soren Kierkegaard in the nineteenth-century said "I have identified two kinds of religion-Religion A and religion B. He said the first is faith in the name only (2 Tim 3:5).

It's the practice of attending church without genuine faith in God and His word. But the religion B (which I believe it is Christianity) on the other hand, is a life-transforming, destiny changing experience which establishes an ongoing personal relationship with God and His word. The word "Religious" came from the word "RELIGIOS" which means back to bondage. Religious is the spirit Satan uses to blind and deceive people.

Religious says we are only going to have peace with God when we get to heaven but what He means when He says my peace I give unto you! John 14:27. What does He mean when He says I will keep you in perfect peace? Isaiah 26:3. Religious say oh God! Show me your glory but what does He mean when He says the glory which thou gives me I have given them? John 17:22.

Religious says we are going to be over comers when we get to heaven but what does He mean when He says in Roman 8:37 "nay in all these things we are more than a conquerors through him who loved us? Is it after death when we leave this earth?

Religious says maybe I will have my healing some day when we go to heaven, what does He mean when He says by His stripes ye were healed? {I Pet. 2:24}, is it after death? Religious says you can't be righteous and be rich at the same time.

What does He mean when He says in II Corinthians 8:9 that Christ became poor for us to be rich? God did not create you to die in poverty. It is possible to know everything about the word of the Lord and still not know the Lord of the word. "The one, who knew no sin, became sin on our behalf that we might become the righteousness of God in Him" {II Corinth. 5:21}. We know the first part is true. But is the last part true? The word of God is your copy receipt of the full payment of what Christ has done for you. This is reality of gospel of Jesus Christ.

A HEART SETTLED WORDS

God is who He says He is (I kings 8:56, Num. 23:19)
You are what God says you are (II Corinth. 5:17, Num. 23:19)
God have what He says He have (Psa. 50:9-11, Psa. 24:1)
You have what God says you have (II Pet. 1:3-4, John 1:12)
God can do what He says He can do (Gen. 18:14. Eph. 3:20)
You can do what God says you can do (Phil. 4:13)
What you don't have means you don't believe, if you can believe as they believed, and act as they acted in the Bible days, you can have the same results as they got in the Bible days.

Note you are a believer and not a doubter, *"if you say who you are, they will say you are proud. And if you don't say who you are, they will say you are not, Say it any way"* said by Rev. Eastwood Anaba (F.G.M).

Even Jesus said who He was by saying I am this, I am that, and What Jesus said to Himself (John 8:12), He said the same thing about us (Math. 5:14). So why don't we say the same words that Jesus said about us? The most dangerous man to the devil is the one who know who he is.

If you don't know who you are, the devil will tell you who you are not. What a wonderful it is to live in the reality of the word, almost all the promises of God has been fulfilled in Christ. No more a promise but a reality. In the New Testament we are born of the word, it is a part of us (I Pet. 1:23, James 1:18). We are the offspring of the word. We don't wait for it to come to pass; it is a part of us now.

CHAPTER 8
ARE YOU THE SELF FALSE PROPHET?

You can be a false prophet over your own life. You are fully responsible nobody else is

_____

-Blessed Prince

Pointing fingers and blaming others as a false prophet has become the other of the day to many. Anytime a false prophet is mention, people think of someone elsewhere with a prophetic gift. I am not saying that there is no prophet or prophetic office in our days.

As far as there are false prophets, it means there are genuine ones. Without the original you cannot find the fake. We have false prophets, false teachers and false brethren, but I want to talk about you. Who are you? Every believer has a grace to prophesy. The truth is you are the prophet of your own life (Job 22:28, Ezekiel 37).

When God said in Joel 2:28 that "your sons and daughters shall prophecy" He meant that everybody in the kingdom will have this ability of God to prophecy, to speak forth God's word and cause it to come to pass.

"No matter who has a word from the Lord for you, if it doesn't confirm what you already have in your own spirit, don't accept it" said by Kenneth Hegin. Each of us is a carrier of a prophetic seed. That's why I feel sorry for those who don't believe in their own words. Prophecy is not only predicting the future but also speaking words with power. Being a prophet does not mean seeing visions and hearing some voices only, but speaking forth the words of God.

The main purpose of every false prophet is to lie, to deceive and to oppose you. Therefore if these three things are found in your life, then you have become a self false prophet unconsciously.

LYING

To lie is not talking the truth. Lying, here I am not talking about lying to others but lying to you.

"They that observe LYING vanities forsake their own mercy" Jonah 2:8 (OKJV)

God is the one who created us, He knows us more than we know ourselves. When he says you are blessed, you are blessed, when he says you are healed, you are healed. You don't need to feel it or see it with your physical eyes. Doubting God's word makes Him a liar but the Bible says God *is not a liar; let every man be a liar and God, a true'* (Rom. 3:4).

So if God has said something, and you say something else, then you've been a liar. You've made yourself a false prophet over your own life! Receive grace to understand!

DECIEVE

"Let no man deceive himself".....I Corinth. 3:18a. It is possible for a man to deceive his own self or heart (spirit).The word "heart" in the Bible is the same as spirit and God guides us through our spirit (Prov. 20:27)

"But be the doers of the word and not hearers only, DECEIVING YOUR OWN SELVES (own heart)". James 1:22, 26

The word deceive came from the Greek word **"PLANAO"** which means to lead astray. To deceive yourself is to programmed yourself by negative words and information whiles expecting good to come but that cannot be. Many have a lot of reasons to fail in anything but not a reason to win or become successful in life.

Any word that enters into you will either form or deform you. Jesus said **"Take heed of the words you hear. {**Mark 4:24} because words are spirits {John 6:63}. Consistently speaking failure, sickness and poverty, you have condition yourself for that way of life; you may wish for a better and good life, and sought for it with tears; all money in the bank can be giving to you and still end up broke. Why! Because your spirit can only process poverty, lack and sickness, instead of prosperity and good health. Anytime you deceive yourself, you stand in as a false prophet in your own life!

OPPOSE

It is natural for every living thing to grow. So it is to the believer, whether in ministry, business or anywhere you found yourself in life. *But the path of the just is as shining light, that shineth and more unto the perfect day (Prov. 4:18).* As a child of God you are not permitted to stand still in life. I know there are spirits that can oppose people. But Paul said, someone can oppose his own self, without any spirit involved at all. See

"In meekness instructing THOSE THAT OPPOSE THEMSELVES, if God peradventure will give them repentance to acknowledging of the truth, and that they may recover themselves out of the snare of the devil, who are taken captive by him (Satan) at his (your) will' II Timothy 2:25-26 (KJV).

To be opposed means to stand against or to be restricted. This is one of the strategies the devil is using in destroying people. He causes them to work against themselves by overthrowing it through their wrong confession. Don't deny yourself of every good things, because your heavenly father knows that you need them (Math. 6:32). Stop pretending; also you can bewitch yourself without any witch (Gal. 3:1).

God is not going to hold any body responsible when misled, because He has given us the Holy Spirit and his word to discern. By your words you will either act like God or like the devil. It is up to you. Receive a fresh revelation in the name of Jesus! Satan is after your word to have them in order to operate against you.

CHAPTER 9
YOUR MOUTH IS A WEAPON

God knows that you will have enemies and the most effective weapon he gave to you is your mouth _____

-Blessed Prince

Everything good has an enemy. Even Jesus had enemies, so you will have enemies throughout your entire life. Battles are real to life, whether you believe it or not but triumph are even more real to the believer. Every battle has its strategies and you can win if you follow the divine instructions to avoid tragedies. *"Christianity is a warfare, when you don't lose the battle inside you cannot lose it outside" said by Arch-Bishop Benson Idahosa of blessed memory*. When God created man, He said take dominion; it means there are things that will try to oppose you. And it is either you dominate them or they dominate you. Your mouth is a dangerous weapon of the battles of life, which can work for or against you, depending on how you use it.

"And he had in his right hand seven stars, AND OUT OF HIS MOUTH WENT A SHARP TWO-EDGED SWORD and his countenance was the sun shines in his strength" Revelation 1:16

The Greek word translated "mouth actually means "the front or edge of a weapon. William Shakespeare said "my voice is my sword". When you open your mouth and begin to speak words in faith you are using your weapon of war given to you by God to establish your liberty on earth. Even Jesus, with all his messianic anointing had to speak aloud to the devil; He had to use his mouth to free Himself from the devil's trap (Mark 8:33). The truth is you are God's battle axe and weapons of war on earth to destroy the works of the devil.

"You are my battle axe and weapons of war: for with you will I break in pieces the nations: and with you will I destroy kingdoms, and with you will I break in pieces the horse and his rider. And with you will I break in pieces the chariot and his rider. Jeremiah 51:20-20.

TAME YOUR ENEMIES

God says He has made you a god over your pharaoh {Exodus 7:1}. Some people believe that the devil is very powerful and as a result they always try to avoid talking about him. "If I don't bother the devil, he won't bother me" but that's wrong, you have to be on the offensive against the devil before he starts messing things up around you. As a Christian, you are to constantly launch an onslaught against the enemy. The best way to defend is to attack said by Pastor Richard Atiayao (Winners Chapel Int.). It's also very important for you to realize that you may not get whatever you desire just because it's written in the Bible. There are forces out there working to keep you from possessing those things which are legally yours in Christ. But the Bible says

"You have also GIVEN ME THE NECKS OF MY ENEMIES, so that I will destroy those who hate me". Psalm 18:40

"The Lord shall send the rod of your strength out of Zion, RULE IN THE MIDST OF YOUR ENEMIES". Psalm 110:2

Even God knows that you have an enemy ad that's why He gave you a mouth. Psa. 8:2. You can't be too gentle and become a conqueror; it takes manliness to subdue opposition. We have been too busy talking to God for many years, but a time has come for us to learn how to talk to situations and to the oppositions **now**!

To keep your mouth shut in battle is to shut yourself in as a captive. It is your heritage right to condemn every tongue that rises up against you; else it will prevail against you {II Thessalonians 1:6, Isaiah 54:17}. If you don't force it to pass, it will force you to pass. To be ignorant of Satan's strategies is to a victim of tragedy!

"For I will give you a mouth and wisdom, which ALL YOUR ADVERSARIES SHALL NOT BE ABLE TO GAINSAY NOR RESIST". Luke 21:15.

God didn't give your enemies the final say. Gainsay means if your voice does not supersede your enemies, you have not started living yet, because your enemies will always try to silence you. Until the enemies hear your voice they will not obey you (Psa. 18:44-45, II Corinth. 10:4-5). There is no excuse for any believer to be defeated. Your victory is guaranteed in every sphere of life. Listen, If Jesus need your permission before He can enter your life (Rev. 3:20), then who is the devil to enter into your life without your permission? Receive a revelation right now in the name of Jesus!

THE DEVIL IS UNDER YOUR CONTROL

A Christian has the very nature and the life of God, so Satan has no power over him. When you are well taught you cannot be trapped. To know your position in Christ is very important. We don't live by our condition but by our position.

"And has raised us up together, AND MADE US SIT TOGETHER IN HEAVENLY PLACES in Christ Jesus". Ephesians 2:6

The Christian is not under servitude to the devil. You are seated in heavenly places in Christ not by your making but by the power of His grace. You are in the place of authority with Christ, far above Satan and everything connected to him, you are superior to Satan. In heavenly places, Satan has no power to prevail (Rev. 12:7-9). We live in two realms at the same time, when you come to this awareness, the devil cease to be your problem. Don't appeal or beg the devil, command him. He is under your feet. The Bible said

"And the God of peace shall bruise Satan UNDER YOUR FEET SHORTLY, The grace of our Lord Jesus Christ be with you. Amen! Romans 16:20.

There is an organizational hierarchy in every institution. Instructions is taking from above to below not from the below to above. The reason the devil is still giving you a command is because you have not put him where he belongs. You have placed him so highly that God has no choice but to leave him where you have put him. The place you give is where he will occupy (Eph. 4:27).God will only deal with the enemy that is under your feet, because that is where God will bruise him.

Demons are spiritual beings and they only respond to words that are spiritual. Satan is dethroned and the way he exercise control over men's life is through their ignorance. If Satan has any authority of his own, he would not have to depend on deception. The secret of all successful warfare lies in the mouth. It is a time for you to stop the stopper, break the breaker, destroy the destroyer and kill the killer.

CHAPTER 10

REAL FAITH GOES WITH CONFESSION

The connection between your heart and your mouth has been joined together by God; let no man put it asunder!

-Blessed Prince

Remember that faith is not some rigid demand that causes God to bow to the believer's whims, but rather a principle in the kingdom by which the believer connects with God covenant words and God perform His word in their live.

"But the righteous which is of faith speaks in this way, do not say in your heart, who will ascend into heaven? [that is, to bring Christ down from above].Or who shall descend into the abyss? [that is, to bring up Christ from the dead].But what does it say? The word is near you, EVEN IN your MOUTH, AND IN YOUR HEART. That is the word of faith, which we preach. That if you shall confess with your mouth the Lord Jesus, and shall believe in your heart that God has raise Him from the dead, you will be saved. For with heart man believes unto righteousness, and with the mouth confession is made unto salvation." Roman 10:6-10

Apostle Paul, through the spirit wrote a letter to explain what faith really means in the New Testament to the people in Rome. He shows them that there is no distance in the spirit when it comes to faith. He quoted them from the Book of Deuteronomy 30:12-14 and told them that, they don't need to see Christ Jesus personally or with their physical eyes before they can be saved. All they need is to believe with their heart that God has raised Him from the dead and confess it with their mouth unto salvation. Just believing it in your heart will not make the work done, you need to confess what you believe in your heart to make it done.

BELIEVE IS NOT FAITH

Faith does not believe and believing is not faith. Faith believes and corresponding action put together.

"You believe that there is one God, You do well, and the devils also believe and tremble. But do you know, o foolish man, that faith without works is dead? James 2:19-20

Faith start with believing but you must not stop at merely accepting what the word says; you must take a step further by making a confession or taking an action. Any faith that does not grow to a level of confession is a lie, a cheat, a fraud and fake. God has never given any attention to it or His angles.

The Bible has not once mentioned it at all but only the speaking faith David said I believe, therefore I have spoken. Paul quoted him in II Corinthians 4:13 and said "we also believe and therefore speak. Why that "therefore?" because genuine faith and confession of your mouth are absolutely essential to the existence of each other.

Do not forget that believing with your heart and confessing with the mouth stand closely connected and what God has joined together let no man put asunder!

God has never given any attention to faith that doesn't express itself. From Genesis to this hour, dumb faith, Say-nothing faith, Cowards faith does not have attention of God. Faith is a living force draw from the living word to produce living proves.

Faith is not the denial of facts but denying those facts, the ability or authority to control the circumstance of your existence (Rom.4:19-20). Faith is living beyond your situation by the word. It is the lifestyle of the Just. (Heb. 10:38). The just shall not live by friends, funs or family but by faith. God only respond to your faith not your tears or circumstance.

Faith is the force that reaches out into the unreality of things you need into the world of the spirit (heaven supply) into physical manifestation. It is words that make faith complete.

CHAPTER 11
THE DANGER OF DOUBLE CONFESSION

The most dangerous of all confession is double confession. It will be good not to confess at all _____

-Blessed Prince

There is a grave danger of double confession and the cause of it is a double minded. A double minded man is unstable in all his ways (James 1:8), not some of his ways but all his ways. He is unstable (unsettled), he is driven and tossed by every winds of life. The reason is that his mind will control his choice of words and his words will ultimately control his life.

That is why David said**… "I have purposed that my mouth shall not transgress"** (Psa. 17:3). He refused to make a double confession. Jesus knew the danger of double confession that is why He warned us about it.
"But let your communication BE, YES, YES; NO, NO; for whatsoever is more than these comes from the evil one". Matthew 5:37

God doesn't use empty figures Of speech. He means what He says! You heard somebody shouting I am healed and today when he feels the pains, he says "I am sick. You hear him say. "I am rich and when things aren't so good, you will hear him say "I am so broke" The second statements has destroy the first one. When you do this you frustrate the grace of God. When you say one thing and mean the opposite, that's flattery, you are flattering God yourself, and "A flattering mouth makes a ruin (Prov.26:28).

They are like the children of Ephraim who being armed and carrying bows yet turned back in the day of battle (Ps 78:9). And when that happens, vacillate spirit has taken over. To vacillate means to be undecided or wavering about something. It is a confuse spirit, the Bible calls it staggering. Abraham didn't stagger at God's promise and being fully persuaded that, what He had promised, He is able also to perform (Rom. 4:21), He didn't say one thing today and another thing tomorrow.

Positive confession dominates circumstance, while vacillating confession permits circumstance to govern one. In the realm of the spirit it is not allowed to have a double confession, and when you do that your life will be out of order. This is what makes prophet Isaiah to say that

"These also WHO ERRED IN SPIRIT will come to understanding, and those who complained will learn doctrines". Isaiah 29: 24. (KJV)

Do not erred in the spirit but have a discipline spirit to maintain your confession no matter what is going on in the physical; it has no root over you. The penalty for wavering in our confession is that we deny ourselves of the power of God's word {Luke 9:62}. This is the reason Angel Gabriel made Zacharias a mute and he didn't speak until the day the things he said came to pass. (Luke 1:17). Because Zacharias has power in his words, and negative confession from him can stop what God want to do in his life. When you speak hold on to that. Once you speak positive creation begins and when you speak negative destruction happens to what you have created in the spirit. Don't talk the circumstance; speak the end result of what you want.

Don't talk about sickness because you feel the pain in your body! Trust Gods word than what you feel. Notice that Jesus' body was buried in the tomb without any blood, because the soldier pierced His side with spear and all the blood of His body gushed out {John 19:34}. He was raise up by the Holy Spirit and walked on the street of Jerusalem for 40 days without blood in His body, this is a proof that man shall not live by the bread alone.

The Bible says "If the spirit that raised Jesus from the dead dwell in you, the same spirit shall vitalize your body" {Rom. 8:11}. Therefore the total vitality of the believer's body is not only depends on the food he eat but by the spirit of God that is within him.

IT MUST NOT BE SO

"Out of the same mouth proceeded blessing and cursing. My brethren, THESE THINGS OUGHT NOT SO TO BE. Does a spring send forth fresh water and bitter from the same opening? Can the fig tree, my brethren bear olives, or grapevine bear figs? Thus no spring yields salt water and fresh". James 3:10-12

Beloved, to know more about the danger of double confession, you need to study this scripture from verse 2-14. Do you know that when you hear yourself say something?

It has a huge impact on your own mind and heart. God knows this and the devil knows this also. That is why they both want you to speak words that agree with their plans for your life. If you speak the devil's words, you will get the devil's plan. And if you speak God's word, you will get God's plan.

Anytime you confess disease, weakness and failure, you magnify the adversary above God and your own confidence in the word. And anytime you confess healing, strength and victories, you place the devil where he belongs. Many believers failed when things becomes difficult because they stops their right confession.

When you confess negatives, it is because you believe in it more than the positives. For the Bible says *"Out of the abundance of the heart the mouth speaks"* (Matt. 12:34)

Peoples, who are joyous, fulfilled and whose lives are full of great things are those who have been talking that way. When you talk more of negative things you don't want, unconsciously you are drawing more of it into your life. Stop that and replace them with the positive ones. You have to talk about the good things you want to bring into your life.

ISAAC'S INSIGHT

Isaac knew the danger of double confession that is why he couldn't reverse his blessing from Jacob or to curse him when he finds out that he has been deceived. He has already blessed him by saying cursed be every one that cursed thee and blessed be everyone that blessed thee" (Gen. 27:29). So for him to cursed Jacob is to curse himself! The Bible says *"so speak and so act, as those who are to be judged by the law of liberty" (Jms 2:12).*

To say one thing today and say another thing tomorrow means you are in bondage! A person who has liberty speaks as a free man and does not change his words. This is the reason you have to maintain your confession of God's word, (Heb. 4:14) in spite of everything. When you confess in consonance with God's word consistently, angels will be activated on your behalf and attract to you things you desire.

"The wise man shall be known by his good confession (James3:13). **And to him that ordered his conversation and aright will I show the salvation of God"** {Psa. 50:23}.

Wrong confession will cost your victory, prayer answers, money and if you are not careful, it can cost you your life. *"He that swear to his own hurt AND CHANGES NOT will not be move"* **(PS. 15: 4).** The same thing goes to those who swear to their own good, peace, health, prosperity and changes not. NO MORE DOUBLE CONFESSION IN JESUS NAME!

CHAPTER 12
THE 7 MYSTERIES OF CONFESSING GOD'S WORD

There are mysteries in this kingdom and the kingdom mysteries is given to us to dominate the world

-Blessed Prince

Satan operate in a mystery called "The mystery of iniquity" {2 Thess. 2:7}, and God's answer to the mystery of iniquity is "The mystery of godliness". [I Tim 3:16]. It takes mystery to overcome mystery. But thank God, there is a higher mystery on our side. The church is moving from doctrines into mysteries {Eph. 3:1-5}.

The word mystery came from the Greek Word "MUSTERION" which means unveiling the hidden things, secrets or discovery. Listen to what Jesus said to His disciples about mystery

"He answered and said unto them, because IT IS GIVEN UNTO YOU to know the mysteries of the kingdom of heaven, but to them it is not given". Matthew 13:11.

Christianity is all about discovering the hidden things of God by His spirit to differentiate us from the rest of the world. *Bishop David O. Oyedepo once said "The Bible stories don't change life but the Bible mystery does". How true it is!*

Mysteries are wrapped in Biblical simplicity but you will never know until the spirit revealed it to you. Anytime you speak the word something happen, whether you know it or not. The Bible says

"You have heard; see all this. AND WILL YOU NOT DECLARE IT? I have made you hear new things from this time, Even HIDDEN things, and you did not know them. They are created now and not from the beginning; And before this day you have not heard them, lest you should say, 'of course I knew them". Isaiah 48:6-7.

What God is saying here is, this is a mystery you don't know, when your ear hears this and when your eyes see that the moment you speak you start creating things, you will not stop speaking. Prophet Samuel knew these mysteries, no wonder not one of his words fall into the ground. (I Sam. 3:21). Hallelujah!

- **YOU TURN INTO ANOTHR MAN**

"Then the spirit of the LORD will come upon you, and you will prophesy with them, AND BE TURNED INTO ANOTHER MAN". I Samuel 10:6

Remember that as you speak forth the word concerning you under the anointing, you are prophesying. You can't drive a car unless, you are a driver. So it is in the spirit, you can't do something unless you become it to do it. *John. G. Lake said "the secret of heaven's power was not in just doing but in the being, when you become the being the doings are normal".*

Samuel said to Saul, I have told you everything about your life in the spirit, but unless you speak it, you will remain the same as you are and die the same as you are. Therefore say it in order for you to become that man according to the prophesy before you can see it's manifestation in your life. Becoming another man means trans-formation and the word "Trans" means living above your location. Thank you the spirit of God!

- **YOU BECOME A WONDER**

"And it happened, when all who knew him formerly saw that he indeed prophesied among the prophets, that the people said one to another "what is this that has come upon the son of kish? IS SAUL ALSO AMONG THE PROPHETS?" I Samuel 10:11

It means people cannot predict you and they cannot deny your effect {Act 4:13-16}, David also said "you **have make me a wonder to my generation** "{Psa. 71:7}. May people take note of you from today and may you become a wonder in the name of Jesus!

- **IT LEVITATE YOU TO A HIGHER PLACE**

"And when he had finished an end of prophesying, HE CAME TO THE HIGH PLACE". I Samuel 10:13

The high place here means to be positioned in life where things will be under your control. It means you can't hide in life. No matter what the enemies will do or ever do you will stand tall (Math. 5:14).

"Then you delight yourself in the LORD; and I will cause you to ride on the HIGH PLACES OF THE EARTH, and feed you with the heritage of Jacob your father. The mouth of the LORD has spoken". Isaiah 58:14

Remember He said it so that you may say something. You are coming out of obscurity into lime light. You belong to the top only and not the below!

- **YOU ESTABLISH YOUR DESTINY**

"Forever O Lord thy word is SETTLED (Establish) in heaven"-Psalm 119:89.

It says the word is settled in heaven not in earth or in your life; therefore it is your responsibility to settle it in your life here on earth. Job said.... *"Receive instruction from His mouth and ESTABLISH HIS WORDS IN YOUR HAERT" (Job 22:22).*

This is what many Christians don't know. To establish the scriptures you read from the Bible into your life, saying it is very important. God gave instruction to Moses to tell His children that

"Say unto them, as truly as I live says the Lord as ye have spoken in my ears, SO WILL I DO TO YOU". Numbers 14:28

Joshua and Caleb established their destiny for positive by their mouth. Notice the words "as you have spoken in my ears, so I will do to you "God is saying in effect you have settled what I will do to you by the words you have spoken.

- **THE SPIRIT ENTERS YOU.**

There is a spirit behind every word (John 6:63) and when you speak, it enters you to cause it to come to pass in your life.

"Then THE SPIRIT ENTERED me when He spoke to me, and set me upon my feet; and I heard him that spoke to me". Ezekiel 2:2

That's why it's dangerous to hear or says negative words and to sing wrong music as well. (Eccl. 7:5). The question is what spirit do you want to enter you? Receive grace! Spirits also move by words to bring it to pass **"...my mouth has commanded it and his (your) spirit hath gathered them** {Isaiah 34:16}.

- **IT RELAESES FIRE ON YOUR ENEMIES**
"Wherefore thus said the Lord God of host: "Because you speak this word, behold, I will make my words IN YOUR MOUTH FIRE, and this people wood and IT SHALL DEVOUR THEM. " Jeremiah 5:14

It means every chaff of the devil in your life and enemies shall be burn by God's fire, for our God is a God of consuming fire. James said your tongue is fire (Jms 3:6), that also means with your words you can burn up everything your enemies will bring in your life. Paul laid out a fire and a viper came out (Acts 28:6). By a revelation, I decree that any viper in your ministry, business or marriage to be burn and chase out by fire now!

It also convicts people's heart for your favor. The disciples on the Emmaus road said "Did not our heart burn within us, while he talked with us by the way and while he opened to us the scriptures? {Luke 24:32}. From today may people hear your words because they are not empty and have favour with them!

• IT TURNS LOGOS INTO RHEMA WORD

Until the word become Rhema to you, it will not change your situation, Rhema carries power.

"No word from God shall be void of power"-Luke 1:37 ASV.

When the Bible says no word from God shall be void of power "it is not referring to logos word but Rhema word. Logos is the written word of God that expresses his plans, personality, character, purposes and his thoughts. But the Rhema is the active word of God to a specific person, for a specific purpose in a specific time for a specific situation. When you need to effect changes at your work place, your finances, your body or etc., the logos word will not work for you, you need a Rhema word. Logos informs you of what is available to you. But the Rhema shows you how to get it, right words to say at right time for result.

This is the reason some people wonder why they quote scriptures in the face of the devil and nothing happens.

Whatever is not working the way they should in your life is so because you are not prepared to learn how to make it work. It is not that such things cannot work; you have not made yourself available to learn how to make them work. They fail to realize that it is not just quoting of scriptures that produce result, even the devil quotes scriptures, but receiving Rhema from that scripture you are quoting is what makes it work. That's what causes the devil to bow before you.It is the sound code of the spirit (Rhema), as Ezekiel said "I prophesy as I was commanded".

The Bible says who is he that speaks and comes to pass when the lord has not commanded it (gives Rhema)? Lam 3:37.Rhema comes by meditation and the repetitions of the scripture till your spirit catch the revelation.

Remember that everybody can preach the word but not everybody can minister the word in the spirit; and everybody can hear the word but not everybody can listen or receive it in the spirit. {Rev. 3:6 and Math. 19:11}. Jesus said, there were ten bridegrooms, all of them have a title of virgin yet it was only the five of them who are wise (Math. 25). Everybody can have a title as minister but …….. Think about it.

CHAPTER 13
THE UNSPEAKABLE WORDS (COMMUNICATING IN HEAVENLY LANGUAGE)

Until you come to a level of speaking like God; you can't function like Him

-Blessed Prince

Every area of life has a language and only those who understand the language can succeed therein. The earth has it language and the heaven also has it language. Even on the earth we have different kind of languages. E.g Doctors has their language, lawyers have theirs, military and police have theirs. Have you ever seen a doctor's note or prescription sheet? Did you really understand what he wrote? I know you did not, but take it to the pharmacist and he understands what is written and knows what to do because he knows the medical language. Lawyers also have all kinds of expression, codes and terms that only those in the profession understand. In same way God want His children to know and understand how to communicate in heavenly language.

God knows every language on this earth but He doesn't communicate to us through our earthly language. For instance, if you are a Chinese and understands English, when an English man is talking, you can hear and understand him in your language even though he is not speaking Chinese. That is the same way God does to us. Because in the spirit we don't have any Anglophone or Francophone, any Spanish or Greek; there are no language barriers. The best way to have great relationship is to be able to communicate in the person's language and to his level. Words are the conduit for the greatest power in the universe, the more spiritual we become, and the more we will understand this. That is why Paul said,

"However, WE SPEAK (Gk "Laleios") WISDOM among the mature ("Teleios"), yet not the wisdom of this age, nor of the ruler of this age, who are coming to nothing. But we speak the wisdom of God in a mystery, the hidden wisdom, WHICH GOD ORDAINED BEFORE THE AGE (world) FOR OUR GLORY; which none of the rulers of this age knew; for had they known, they would not have crucified the Lord of glory…........ But God has revealed them to us through His spirit: for the spirit searches all things, yes, the deep things of God. ...... Which things we also speak, not in the words which man's wisdom teaches but which the Holy Spirit teaches; comparing spiritual things with spiritual. But the natural man does not receive the things of the spirit of God: for they are foolishness to him: nor can he know them, because they are spiritually discerned". Corinthians 2:6-8, 10, 13-14

Paul explained the importance of understanding and speaking spiritual words (language). As those texts also declares. God knows that it could be easy to communicate to us in our own earthly language? The question is, why doesn't He speak to us in our language? He has a good reason and not to confuse us, but to teach us the language of the spirit to operate and function in His level, with words which is

74

much greater, far more expressive, accurate and powerful than any language of men, because our earthly language has a limit.

THE UNSPEAKABLE WORDS

"I knew a man in Christ about fourteen years ago (whether in the body, I cannot tell or whether out of the body I cannot tell. God knoweth) such a one caught up to the third heaven. And I knew such a man (whether in body or out of the body, I cannot tell God knoweth). How that he was caught up into paradise AND HEARD UNSPEAKABLE WORDS which it is not lawful for a man to utter" Corinthians 12:2-4 OKJV.

When you read this text further you will know that Paul was actually talking about himself. The unspeakable words are not just tongues. Even the one who interprets tongues is greater than the one who speaks it. The unspeakable words are words that transcend human words. It is the same as communicating in heavenly language. They are words that are beyond human understandings (mental capacity or reasons). Paul said it was not lawful for men to utter. Not lawful here means, it was not proper for men to speak on earth here. Because if you do men will see you as abnormal person. You need to know that there is a big difference between the ways heavens communicate and the way earthly communicate.

Jesus came to live the heavenly life on earth and to show us how to communicate heaven language on earth, but the people were confused about his words. He had this awareness that in heaven nobody dies, so He told His disciples that Lazarus has fallen asleep, so they should go and wake him up. They couldn't understand, until He came to their levels in the way of earthly communicate, by saying he is dead (John 11:11-14).

Jesus was not out of reality, He was showing them how to communicate in heavenly language. He was expressing the reality of the situation better than anybody could realize in heaven's view. If He says Lazarus is dead, He is saying that it is over, that nobody will be able to wake him up. But if He say he is sleeping; He have altered the response to the situation, so let's go and wake him up.

In Luke 8:50-56, Jesus entered one of the rulers of the Synagogue's house to raise his dead daughter, He told them that she is not dead but she sleep, they laughed Him to scorn and said to one another, this man is mad. You must know the difference between the two (heaven and earthly language).

A rich man once said that, whiles they were growing up his father told them that the difference between the rich and the poor is the way they use their words. So his father forbids them not to say words like,

"I am nothing"

"I can't do it"

"I can't afford it"

"It is too expensive"

"What if I fail?"

I believe that is the same way God want to train us. There is no I can't in the Bible. Men were not made to say negative words, what they see or feel but to talk what they want to see and feel. Confession is re-echoing what God has said.

Example of unspeakable words are "Let the weak say I am strong" {Joel 3:10}. "The inhabitants shall not say I am sick" {Isaiah 33:24}. He is not telling you to lie, because the more you keep on saying the things as they are, the more you will have them. Therefore you say boldly, I cannot be sick in Jesus name! You say I cannot be poor {2Corith. 9:8-9}. You say I have overcome the world; greater is He that is in me than the one which is in the world {I John 4:4-5}.

You say God shall supply all my need according to His riches (Phil 4:19).In this world we receive first before we give thanks. But in heaven we give thanks first before we see its manifestation (John 11:4, Psa. 50:23, and Psa. 67:5-7). Someone might say 'but people are going to think I am a strange, yes! The world cannot receive this because it is foolishness unto them, but it is the wisdom of God for our glory [I Corinth. 2:14]. Learning the right communication is a part of spiritual growth in Christianity.

WHEN NATURAL MEN TALKS THEY MAKE SENSE, BUT WHEN THE SPIRITUAL MAN TALKS HE DOESN'T MAKE SENSE BUT THEY MAKE EFFECT!

What a miracle change would be produced in the church today if her members would rise to the place God desires His chosen ones to talk.

CHAPTER 14
OUT OF THE SHADOWS

Those who look at the sun do not see shadows and shadows lookers always miss the reality

-Blessed Prince

A few months ago I was listening to a preacher on T.V and he was saying that any pastor who will tell you that God has blessed you or will bless you is a liar. With seriousness on his face, he said this is because God has cursed all mankind but after he finished everything, he contradicted himself by saying "may God bless you". How can the same God who has cursed all mankind bless someone? Is He who told us to choose blessing and not curse {Deut. 30:19}. How can God curse a man who He has already blessed? This is strange but that is what many have believed.

You see, the Old Testament is walking in the shadows and the New Testament gives us true light to see the hidden parts of that shadows. Remember that shadows don't talk, only the reality. Paul said "we all with an open faces look through the darkly glass". In the Old Testament, they see through the darkly glass. So they were operating according to the parts of their revelations given to them, until Jesus came to show us the full revelation of God. The big question is, Why God didn't give to the prophets the full revelation of Himself? Because they can't take it and also it was God's purpose that His fullness be located in Christ bodily (Col. 2:9)

"In many SEPARATE REVELATION (each of which set forth a portion of the truth) and in different ways God spoke of old to (our) forefathers in and by the prophets (but) in the last of these days he has spoken to us in (the person of a) Son, whom he appointed heir and lawful owner of all things, also by and through whom He created the worlds and the reaches of space and the ages of time (He made, produced, built, operated and arranged them in order) He is the sole expression of the glory of God (the light being-being, the out-raying of the divine) and He is the perfect imprint and very image of (God) nature ...."
Hebrew 1:1-4 Amp

There were some revelations that were separated for only Jesus. That is why He sounds controversial to them. He said "you have heard that" and "had heard this" but "I say this or I say unto you". Because the whole scroll was mixed-up, and He came to divide them rightly, and to arrange them in its proper order. So the prophets were operating in the lesser truth and Jesus came with the greater truth. You can see it clearly in Matthew5:38-48.

God did not curse Adam when he committed the high treason! You may be surprise!! He cursed the serpent and the ground instead of Adam, read Genesis 3:14-19 carefully. He also said in Genesis 8:21 as a confirmation that He cursed the ground and not the man. *"God said in His heart, I will not curse the ground any more for man's sake"* Why not the man but the ground? Because it is a spiritual law that you can't curse a blessed man. God has already blessed them in Genesis 1:28; And the Bible says God is eternal and whatsoever He doeth, it shall be forever {Eccl. 3:14}.So to curse them will be a contradiction to Himself and His word, also that curse will be eternal.

Miles Coverdale, who translated and produced the first English Bible said something I like most, he said " it shall greatly help thee to understand scriptures, if thou mark not only what is spoken or written, but of whom and unto whom, with what words at what time, where, to what intent, with what circumstance. Considering what goes before and what followed after, when you read the Bible unless you are left with a "con" and I add to it that if you see or read anything that's not in consistency of God's character, take note. Even in Amos 3:6 say

"If there is evil in the city, the Lord has done it". And I Samuel 16:14 says *"But the spirit of the Lord departed from Saul and an evil spirit from the Lord troubled him".*

 How can evil spirit come from the Lord?

From these two verses it seems like

1) God permit evil, but James said God does not tempt anybody with evil.2) It seems like God possesses two spirits (good and evil) and when you do good, He gives you the good spirit and when you do evil, He replace it with evil spirit. How can it be possible? Know that every word in the Bible is truly stated but not every word in the Bible is a statement of truth. Thank God for Dr. Robert E. Young, the Hebrew and Greek scholar who came out to straighten this issue

First, you need to understand the style and manner of communication of the prophets in the Old Testament, and extent of the revelation granted to them. The prophets knew nothing about Satan except in figurative speech, because there was no revelation of him. To them, everything that happened, whether good or evil, came from God. Jesus made an enlightening statement to the Pharisees in Mathew 19:8. He said "Because of the hardness of your heart,......but in the beginning it was not so". Which means God allow Moses to say certain things because of the hardness their heart. If it is not true that an evil spirit can come from God, then is not true that God cursed Adam, for He is not the originator of curse!

Now let's come to the point. The question is, would you curse your children when they disobey your instructions? **No**! Even Isaac, as a man as he was couldn't curse Jacob when he found out that he has been deceived [Gen27:1-39]. Don't you think that God knows better than Isaac? The Bible says "Bless and curse not" (Rom. 12:14). Remember that it was Moses who received the revelation of the Genesis. And the Bible says in John 1:17 that

"For THE LAW WAS GIVEN through Moses, but GRACE and TRUTH came through Jesus Christ". John 1:17

So Moses rates everything by the law, for that was what he received. Moses was having the shadow or the fact but Jesus brought the reality or the truth. Even Moses did not say God curse man. Therefore we need the greater light or truth in the New Testament to locate the hidden truth, and that must be found in the mouth of Jesus.

"If yon then, being evil, KNOW HOW TO GIVE GOOD GIFTS TO YOUR CHILDREN, HOW MUCH MORE WILL YOUR HEAVENLY FATHER give not the Holy Spirit to those who ask HIM!" Luke 11:13

And also in James 1:17 says "Every good and perfect gift cometh from above and cometh down from the father of lights. With whom is no variableness, neither shadow of turning".

Curse is not part of the good things. You may say the first scripture is talking about the Holy Spirit. Thank you sir! BUT what did Jesus said about the Holy Spirit? He said when the Holy Spirit comes, He will guide you into all truth, not some but all (John 16:13).

It means there are some truths of God that is still hidden in the scriptures and His job is to reveal them to you.

Never allow the sentiment to destroy revelation. The question is, "Where did the curse and the death came from in the first place?" It did not come from God, but it came from the fruit they ate. Because the root of the devil was in it. What God actually did was to announce to them the outcome of what they have done! I am not trying to say that there is no curse, but even if there is a curse, the Bible says Christ has become a curse for us, so that the blessing of Abraham might come into our lives. (Gal. 3:13-14). Remember, that shadows don't talk but only the reality.

CHAPTER 15
BLESS YOURSELF

The first thing God did for man is to blessed them, and the last thing you will ever do is to curse yourself. You are legally blessed, therefore any curse that comes to your life are illegal

-Blessed Prince

Legally you are blessed by God, therefore any curse that comes your way are illegal. Men began his life in a blessing and must end his life in blessing. Before sin came, there was blessing, before curse there was a blessing, and before death there was a blessing. When God blessed man the devil was not there, therefore we must reject anything that looks like a curse. It is very important to be blessed by your pastor, influential persons and your parents. Many destinies are drying up because there is no anointed mouth speaking into their lives. Also parents should come to this awareness that you can give everything to your children, with a good education and still end up as nothing. Because words are important in their lives and it is your responsibility to release words of blessing into their lives on a daily basis.

Time has proven that people tend to live up the words upon their lives. Some parent calls their children stupid, fool, block head, good for nothing, because of the way they see them behave and later they wonder why things are not working for their children. No! Call them what you want to see from them. May be your parents died without blessing you or someone has cursed you one way or the other, Hear me "Don't give up on yourself", don't curse yourself. Anyone who is cursing you whether in public or secret, even if it is in their mind, has already cursed themselves because you are blessed by God Himself! Remember that every curse is a reversible. The only person that can keep God's blessing from you is yourself. Whatever happens to you, God always speaks to you on how to do it the better way. No evil has power over you; you have all the power for good. Don't allow anybody's negative words to entangle you. Do something to it, speak back. Remember that if you have a mouth, you have a choice. The Bible says

".....you will also decree a thing, and it will be established for you, so light will shine on your ways". Jobs 22:28

You see, good understanding gives favour (Prov. 13:15) and we live by favour not by labour. Favour is not fair but fabulous. Remember, not everybody will accept you, even they did that to Jesus and called him by names (John 1:11, Matt. 21:42). Consider everyone's comments as their own opinion and make sure you are not what they called you. The only permission God has given to everybody in your life is to bless you and not to curse you. If they do otherwise, they will end up fighting against God's word (Gen. 12:3). Bless yourself, yes. It is Biblical and you can do that, see it for yourself.

"So [it shall be] that HE WHO INVOKES A BLESSING ON HIMSELF in the land shall do so by saying, may the God of truth and fidelity [the Amen] bless me." Isaiah 65:16 Amp

You can begin from today. Right now, place your hands over your head and begin to bless yourself with words, let it come from your heart. The Holy Spirit is ever ready to use your words to favour you. He cannot use the word except, he uses it through your mouth. And to be filled with the spirit is connected with speaking to yourself (Eph. 5:18-19). Be like prophet Habakkuk who pick his stringed instruments and started blessing himself by saying

"Although the fig tree shall not blossom, nor fruit be on the vines; Though the labour of the olive may fall, and the fields yield not food; Though the flock may be cut off from the fold, and there be no herd in stalls-Yet I will rejoice in the Lord, I will joy in the God of my salvation. The Lord God is my strength and He will make my feet like deer's feet, and he will make me to walk upon mine high places. To the chief singer on my stringed instruments."Habakkuk 3:17-19.

Declare that you are prosperous and highly favored. Declare that it's impossible for you to be sick, broke or afflicted in the face of contrary winds and adversities, keep talking your way forward. You may say it's easier said than done. No! It is done as you say! When you say it, it is done in the realm of the spirit. It will surely manifest. Select words that will empower bless and raise you (Prov. 18:20, 12:14). The word will never become real to you until you confess it before the world. You must learn to use your mouth to speak God's word consistently, that's what will keep you permanently in the path way of success. Don't forget to keep a confessing list. Your words framed your world for you [Heb. 2:5]. Thank God, that He didn't put your blessing into somebody's hands!

BLESSED IS YOUR NAME

Men give names according to their past, their experience or their family name but God give name according to the vision He has for you. The original name God wants the world to call you is "Blessed not Cursed". "And as your name is, so you are" (II Sam. 25:25). Make no mistake about it. The Bible says

"All nations will call YOU BLESSED, for you will be a delightful land, said the Lord of hosts"
Malachi 3:12

Notice that He said, "ALL NATIONS SHALL CALL YOU BLESSED". If you are called Jacob, don't be offended, but I wonder why people still name their child Jacob, when God Himself changed that name before He was able to blessed him? THINK ABOUT IT. The truth is God didn't call us to use us, but to bless us and to be a blessing to others (Gen. 12:2-5). He said,

"Look unto Abraham your father and Sarah that bore you for I called him alone and BLESSED HIM and increased him" Isaiah 51:2

Can you see that? He called you to bless you and not to use you. Again it says*"....knowing that you ware called to this, that you should INHERIT A BLESSING"- I Peter 3:9.*

Our problem in Christianity is that we are struggling to become blessed, and it is too late for that, because we are already blessed. It is a matter of discovering who you are.

Nobody work for an inheritance, it is a birth right. The question is, shouldn't we work for the Lord? Of course we must work for the Lord. In reality God doesn't want us to work for Him but with Him- in partnership, we are God's follow workers (2 cor 6:1). He did not create men and women to be His servants, but sons and daughters who are whole heartedly involved in running His purpose.

The main purpose of His calling is to bless us. Whatever God does is for your sake and not for His sake. He only uses you for your sake; Because He is not impressed by your works. After all He is God by Himself. When we pray for somebody and they get their healings or miracles, we are only transferring the blessing He has already deposited in us to them. "Freely ye have received, freely give" (Matt. 10:8).

The word "Blessed" came from the Greek word "MAKARIOS" which means to be empowered to succeed in everything, where nothing is missing or broken. Time will never expire such a blessing. God does not only give you blessing but also He makes you a blessing, and being made a blessing is higher than just having a blessing.

"The consciousness of blessing is more powerful than sweating many hours in prayer" Said by Rev. Dr. Robert Ampiah-Kwofi (G.R.M).

You are the blessed of the Lord. Take time to read and meditate on this scripture in Deuteronomy 7: 13-15.

YOU ARE NOT AN ACCIDENT

You are somebody, because God never wasted His time to make a nobody, you may be parental accident, but you are not a divine accident. There is a place for you in the world. Anytime you say negative words about yourself, you have insulted your maker and you set a war within yourself. God brought you to this world by His deliberate design. You are His products and He is your manufacturer, your purpose is determined only through His word. Bless yourself! This is why the psalmist said

"You made all the delicate parts of my body and knit them together in my mother's womb…. YOU SAW ME BEFORE I WAS BORN and scheduled each day of my life before I began to breath, every day was recorded in your book." Psalm 139:13, 16

By this scripture, I have come to know that God doesn't test us to know us, but He test us so that we would know ourselves. Because before He forms you, He knew you. (Jer 1:5). You were not created to be a normal; no one has tour finger prints. Don't allow anyone to cause you to think of yourself as ordinary. There is no one else like you on earth. Your uniqueness was design by God Himself. Whatever makes you feel sorry for yourself or how you are created, places a limit on your destiny. You are not a problem but a solution, those who sees you as a problem doesn't know your worth. YOU WERE BORN TO BE KNOWN FOR SOMETHINGSPECAIL.

You were born to do something that the world will not be able to ignore or to forget. God did not create you to take up space and use up oxygen; you are His carrier of His ideas. You were created as an answer to someone's question and to make a contribution to your generation. From today, if somebody greets and asks how you are? Tell him that God is still blessing you and you are stronger than a metal. Today is the day to concentrate on the blessings of God about your life. When your enemies curse you and people speak evil of you, remember that you are blessed of the lord. In order to manifest it in your life, pray it, think it, talk it, and keep declaring it all the time regardless of the circumstance around you. **BLESS YOURSELF!**

CHAPTER 16
IT IS UP TO YOU

Whenever there's a will, there is a way!

-Blessed Prince

God has already done everything He is ever going to do for you to have a good life, but it is up to you. For instance, Jesus died for all mankind, but not all mankind is saved. You need to confess the lordship of Jesus in your life to make it a reality. So if a man cries out "God, please save me". God the father asks, "Jesus, what is he talking about? Jesus replies "I don't know, I ready redeemed him from his sins, I don't have to go back to earth to die on the cross again, because the price has been paid". Another man cries out to God, "Help, I need money! My life is not making any better! I can't pay my rent and the children's fees! The father looks over and asks, "Jesus, what do you make of this?" Jesus answers, "I don't know, father, I ready pay for the price for his well-being. You see, the issue is no longer what God can do for us. He has already provided for every need. Now the issue is what you and I must do to be more than conquerors.

There are two things that are going on in the Christianity today which I believe it is wrong. It is either they blame God of their problems or the devil. People think it is up to God to do something about their problems. Actually, it is up to you to do something about your problem. Why?, because after Christ's ascension the work that He did in carrying out the great plan of redemption was turned over to the church and now it is up to believers to possess what belong to them. It is not God's responsibility to fulfill His word in your life. While we wait for God to do something for us, God is waiting to work through us! (Eph 3:20, Ezekiel 37).

"Assuredly I SAY UNTO YOU, whatsoever you bind on earth will be bound in heaven and whatever you will loose on earth will be loosed in heaven". Mathew 18:18
The word "Bind" in this scripture also means "forbid" or "disallow" In other words, Jesus is saying…whatsoever thou shall forbid or disallow on earth shall be forbidden or disallowed in heaven. That means you are absolutely responsible for the quality of life you live. God doesn't want good things to happen to you, neither does He mind when bad things happens to you. But He wants you to do good things and when bad things happen to you, He has already given you the power to overcome it. God is allowing whatever you allow.

Do not hold God or even the devil responsible for whatever happens in your life. When you are sick, poor or promoted, it is not the devil that is sick, poor or promoted, it is you. The Bible never told us to pray to God to do something about the devil for us, but it tells us what we should do to the devil. The devil is not a problem! Tell me how many books have been written about the devil in the Bible?

Henry Ward Beecher of the nineteenth-century clergyman said *"Hold yourself responsible for a higher standard than anybody else expects of you. Never excuse yourself, never pity yourself". Be a hard master to yourself and be lenient to everyone else."*God will do it, is the slogan of the indolent. Responsibility means "responding to your ability, we came to the world naked but not empty (2 Corinth. 4:7). Nobody has all but everybody has something. Jesus said

"FOR WHOEVER HAS, to him more shall given and he shell have abundance: BUT WHOEVER DOES NOT HAVE, even what he has shall be taken away from him." Mathew 13:12

Even though this scripture sound so strange and unfair but it is true in the real life. It is those who have, who get even more! But listen, There will never be a day in your life that you will have nothing. God always gives you something to begin your future. You have something and what you have is enough to take you to where you want to be. When you value what you have, your values will be appreciated in life.

DON'T WAIT FOR THE GOVERNMENT
Oh! I feel sorry for anyone who is crying to the government to give them money or to do something that will favor them. God did not put your future into the hands of any government. No government is ever design to make you rich. Haven't you checked the history? Look at Hitler, Sennacherib, Mossolins, Caesars of old and

Stalin who promised the people liberty and prosperity but brought them into bondage. The Bible says they need our help by praying for them (1Tim 2:1). Our lack of prayer to support them has caused the problems we see today.

No great nation is made by a great government; every great nation is a product of great people. Your freedom is within you. *"You are the answer to your problem"* *said by Rev. Asuo Mensah* (Adom F.M)

TALK THE TALK, WALK THE WALK, AND DO THE DO

Have you realized that every time you point an accusing finger at someone, you are pointing three fingers back at yourself, while the fifth one is pointing to God as witness? No more a blaming game! *Life is either a daring adventure or noting-Helen Keller.*

The story of Wilma Rudolph inspires me a lot; she was born prematurely, the twentieth of twenty-two children in a poor family reeling from the impact of the great depression. When she was a child though polio paralyzed both legs, twisting her left foot inward and burdening her with two leg braces, and had to be driven fifty miles twice per week to a hospital for blacks where she receives treatment. In addition, her mother had to rub her legs four times each day for years. At a point, the doctors told her she would never walk, but eventually she proved them wrong. She never stopped dreaming that she would break out of her handicap and succeeded in life, her whole being aspired to triumph over her obstacles, her incredible force of faith and unwavering aspiration to achieve distinction drove her leg nerves and muscles into action.

Astounding everyone, she taught herself to walk, made the basketball team, then became a runner and captured the hearts of fans around the world; by three electrifying Olympic performances in which she brought home three gold medals, the first woman in history to ever do it. The formerly crippled girl became a living legend. She aspired to achievement and nothing could stop her. One of America's great basketball coaches asked her the secret, she replied "WINNING ISN'T EVERYTHING BUT THE WILL TO WIN IS EVERYTHING".

Until you press you cannot be impressed. Nothing can resist the human will that will stake even its existence on its stated purpose. Death isn't the greatest loss in life-the greatest loss is what dies inside of us while we live.

"God made no one for failure, poverty, sickness or shame that everybody is real somebody in God's eyes" said by Dr. T.L Osborn.

Never forget this, riches and wealth are not in things but it is inside you.

Now you can decide the kind of life you want to live. The word decision came from the Latin word "De-caedere". "De" means to form and "Caedere" means to cut. Therefore you can cut any negative things from your life and form it for positive.

Time is not waiting for you. In games, you have extra time but in life you don't have extra time. Get up and take action for what you have been talking for years.

Someone once said "lost wealth may be replaced by industry, lost knowledge by study, lost health by temperance or medicine but lost time is gone forever".

I know that some things do change with time, but times itself change nothing. Things will only change for the worse if left only with time for a change without doing anything.

When you talk and you do not take action, you have made a noise but when you talk and you take action, you make the difference. Dwight D. Eisenhower said *"Neither a wise man nor a brave man lies down on the tracks of history to wait for the train of future to run over him"*. Action is the password for everything. Understanding changes minds, but action changes lives. Therefore waiting for a change without doing anything makes no sense.

Martin Luther King Jnr. Said "if you can't fly, run, if you can't run, walk if you can't walk, crawl but by all means keep moving.

LIFE IS RIDING A BICYCLE, YOU EITHER RIDE ON OR PARK OFF, AND YOU CAN'T STAND STILL. Don't just sit down waiting for heaven to open. Do something to make it open.

Why sitting down waiting for something you can create? Heaven keys are in your hands (Matt. 16:19). Notice your past may be blame on someone but your future may be blame on you, because it is your responsibility. The chief action for a man of spirit is never to be out of action; the soul was never put into the body to stand still. TALK THE TALK, WALK THE WALK, AND DO THE DO.

CHAPTER 17
AFTER CONFESSION

Sometimes the victory does not go to the best, but rather to the one that want it most. If you really want it, you will have it

-Blessed Prince

Satan's first strategy is making us think that God's word is false as he did to the Israelites. The Bible says Pharaoh told his people to make the labour heavier for the Israelites so that they would believe that the word of God concerning their freedom is a lie. See

"Let the labour be heavier on the men, and let them work at it that they may pay no attention to false words" {the word of God to the Israelites}". Exodus 5:9

We must learn to accept this attack when we receive a word from God, not allowing it to discourage us or cause us to deviate from our course.

When a man brings out a product, he puts his label on it to show his confident in the thing. He believes that it will work for his customers. Therefore how can God give you a word which cannot work? Think about it.

"For as the rain comes down and the snows from heaven, and do not return there, but water the earth, and make it bring forth and bud, that it may give

seed to the sewer and bread to the eater. **SO SHALL MY WORD BE** that goes from my mouth. It shall not return to me void. But it shall accomplish that which I please; it shall prosper in the thing whereto I sent it"
Isaiah 55:10-11

- Do not doubt every word you have spoken, even if you are not seeing it manifesting in your life. Your confession of God's word will always come to pass in your life regardless of what opposition Satan puts up against it.(Mark 11:23, EccL. 11:4, James 1:6-8)
- Do not guess how God will do it. Leave the how to God; He is too big to be asking how. (EccL. 11:5, Rom. 10:6-8)
- Keep saying it, until you see its manifesting, his word cannot fail (EccL. 11:3, I Kings. 8:56, Duet 6.6-7).
- Have a spirit of joy. Isaiah 12:3, Phil. 4:4
- Maintain a positive attitude and take action towards that. [Phil. 1:28, Prov. 24:10, James 2:19-20].
- Trust in the Lord. Psalm 37:5, Psalms 34:1.

No matter the storm, with God there's always a rainbow. Read the word, talk the word, confess the word, act on the word and the word will become a part of you. Your mouth will not destroy your destiny any more, but rather it will be a blessing for you in Jesus name!

CONCLUSION

Now you have received the knowledge about the power of confessing God's word that leads to all the good things in life and you will be able to use it to change your entire life. Succeed beyond anything you have ever dreamed before and brings it into reality. The world is waiting for you. My desire is to see every reader of this book at the topmost! **I believe in your future!**

Go and get the part two of this Book entitle CHANGE YOUR WORLD, CHANGE YOUR WORDS! **Since I am a new author, I am accounting on you to introduce this book to one or two people and God will blessed you for doing that.**

      STAY BLESSES YOU.

PRAYER OF SALVATION

I invite you to make Jesus Christ the Lord and savior of your life by praying this prayer.

"O Lord God, I come to you in the name of Jesus Christ, your word say's ....whosoever shall call on the name of the Lord shall be saved" (Acts 2:21). I ask Jesus to come into my heart to be the Lord of my life. I receive eternal life into my spirit and according to Romans 10:9 which says "that, if thou shalt confess with thy mouth the Lord Jesus and shall believe in thine heart that God hath raised him from the dead, thou shalt be saved. I declare that I am saved. I am born again, I am a child of

God. **Thank you Jesus for saving me**

Congratulations! Please let me hear from you.

Contact US on (+233)242654185(+233)268701899

Email: blessedreality2@Gmail.com.

GOD RICHLY BLESSED.

Changing lives, impacting generations through God's word

YOUR MESSAGE IS VERY IMPORTANT TO ME

You are special person to me, and I believe that you are a special to
God. I want to help you in every way i can. Let me hear from you
when you are facing spiritual needs or experiencing a conflict in your
life, or what the lord has done for you by reading this book.
If you want to know that someone cares,

You can write me on my facebook wall: prince Agyapong (Blessed).
Or Email:blessedreality2@gmail.com. Or on whatsApp line:
0268701899.i will pray for your needs and write you back something
i know it will blesses you.

To be a partner with what God is doing in this ministry, your monthly
gift will be a blessing to the kingdom and would bring miracle blessings
into you life. Contact us on +233(0)242654185. God richly bless you.
stay blessed.

-Blessed Prince.

CHANGE YOUR WORLD, CHANGE YOUR WORDS

The world is your estate, it owes you not just a merely living but every good thing you desire. By God's purpose you are the reason for it existence. In yet another riveting masterpiece, Blessed Prince unveils to you that your words are the materials which builds your world. When grace is poured in your lips, you shall be blessed above your Peers. When you begin to realize that the power to do anything, to be anything, and to have anything is within you, only then will you take your proper place to change your world. You can never change your world by being controlled by the earth. **YOUR WORLD IS WAITING FOR YOUR WORD**

THE DANGER OF SIN-CONSCIOUSNESS

The greatest freedom of a man is not political, financial, and physical freedom, but freedom from sin-consciousness. In this outstanding masterpiece, Blessed Prince reveals the mystery of `sin-consciousness and its effects. This has been the heart cry of all men down through the ages. It is better for a man to deny his existence than to let sin consciousness to hold him captive all the days of his life.

Sin-consciousness is dangerous than sin itself. Until your conscience is purged from sins, you can't serve the living God. The devil is not interested in making you to sin than to have sin-conscience.

Unless otherwise identified scripture quotations are from King James (KJV)

Facebook: princeagyapong(blessed).

Instagram-blessedprince

Twitter-blessedprince

Email-blessedreality2@gmail.com

WhatsApp-0268701899

"Speaking God's plan of salvation, the reality of Christ and His blessings for this generation and for next to come"

To be a partner with this ministry, or engagement for preaching, prayers or bulk purchase

Contact us on: (+233) 268701899, (+233) 242654185.

Druck:
Customized Business Services GmbH
im Auftrag der KNV-Gruppe
Ferdinand-Jühlke-Str. 7
99095 Erfurt

FINN'S
THERMAL
PHYSICS